William A.
Barry, S.J.

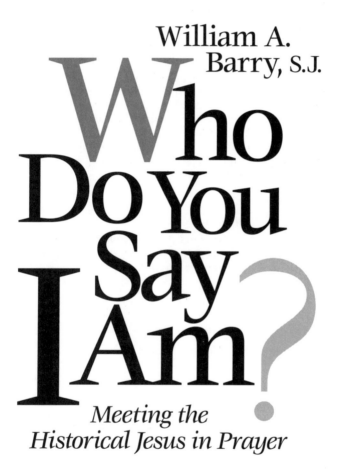

Who Do You Say I Am?

Meeting the Historical Jesus in Prayer

AVE MARIA PRESS Notre Dame, Indiana 46556

International Standard Book Number: 0-87793-579-3
0-87793-570-0 (pbk.)

Cover and text design by Elizabeth Jean French

Printed and bound in the United States of America.

Library of Congress Cataloging-in-Publication Data

Barry, William A.
    Who do you say I am? : meeting the historical Jesus in prayer/ William A. Barry.
    p. cm.
    ISBN 0-87793-575-0 (pbk.)
    1. Jesus Christ—Historicity—Prayer-books and devotions—English.
    I. Title
BT303.2.B256 1996
232.9'08—dc20   95-48160
                                                                      CIP

To
James P. McDavitt, S.J.
Edward P. Babinski, S.J.
and H. Francis Cluff, S.J.
who have served the Jesuits of
the New England province
with uncommon dedication and devotion
and with an unselfish concern for the common
good,
and thus stand for all those Jesuit Brothers
whose unsung labors are often known to God
alone.

Contents

Preface

A couple of years ago Bob Hamma of Ave Maria Press suggested that I try my hand at a book on Jesus that used some of the modern works of Christology. At the time I had no idea what that might mean. Even after I read the first volume of John Meier's *A Marginal Jew* and was moved by the knowledge gained of the historical Jesus, I did not think of writing a book. Then, just as I was beginning Meier's second volume and expecting to finish it at the thirty-fourth General Congregation of the Society of Jesus, I found out that I had a cancerous growth on my vocal cord. The six and one-half weeks of radiation therapy needed precluded my attendance at the Congregation. I had arranged my life and work as provincial so that I would have the months of January, February, and March, 1995, free for the Congregation; now the only thing I had to do was to walk across the street five days a week for a short period of radiation therapy. The radiologist, Dr. Anthony Zeitman, recommended that I do something that would occupy my mind so that I would not focus too much on the treatments. One thing led to another, and I began to write this book.

More than with any other book I have written, the writing of this one took on a prayer dimension. Each time I turned on the computer, I tried to remember to express to Jesus the desire with which I began each chapter: "I want to know more about you so that I may love you more intensely and walk with you more closely." I mention the circumstances to explain the genesis of the book and also its rather personal nature. The circumstances contributed, no doubt, to the particular point of view I take in the book and perhaps to some of the characteristics of the historical Jesus that I stress. In other words, my own situation with its awareness of mortality may have influenced how I read the texts I used in preparing this book. I hope, however, that I have been as true as possible to the results of research on the historical Jesus.

While the first chapter will explain my method, it may not be amiss to expand a little on what this book is about. Since the last century, scholars have tried to sift through the various layers of the New Testament to discover what can be known with some degree of certitude about the actual life and times of Jesus of Nazareth. This work has come to be known as the "search for the historical Jesus." For the most part, during the past century or more the work of these scholars has not impinged much on the beliefs and practices of ordinary Christians. In recent years, however, the search has become a topic for media attention, especially because of the publicity attending the pronouncements of the "Jesus Seminar," a group of scripture scholars who gather periodically to discuss and vote on the "authentic sayings and doings" of Jesus. Some Christians have been shocked by the results of this research, and some have felt their faith shaken. Truth to tell, some of the publicity and some of the "research" has almost seemed calculated to shock.

In my own amateur way I have tried to keep abreast of the scholarly research because I wanted to speak and write from a somewhat solid basic grasp of the scriptures. I did not find my own faith in Jesus shaken. I thought that I might be able to write something that would help others to a deeper knowledge and love of Jesus and to a realization that solid research on the New Testament need not hinder faith, but could contribute to a deeper knowledge and love. I have written with this purpose in mind.

In writing this book I have used John Meier's two-volume work *A Marginal Jew* as my main source. Meier has undertaken a study of the sources to write a reference work on the search for the historical Jesus as part of the Anchor Bible Reference Library, a supplement to the justly famous Anchor Bible Series. It is a monumental task. He has tried to keep his own presuppositions to a minimum and to avoid the trap of reading into the data what he wanted to see. Raymond Brown, S.S., himself one of the great American scripture scholars, states: "When John Meier's work (at least three volumes) is finished it will be the best historical Jesus study produced in the twentieth century" (*An Introduction to New Testament Christology*, 216). Where appropriate and necessary I shall supplement Meier's work with that of other scholars considered equally reliable.

This current work is, understandably, a risk for someone who is neither a scripture scholar nor a professional theologian. Hence I asked Daniel J. Harrington, S.J., editor of *New Testament Abstracts*, scripture scholar and teacher, and best of all, friend, to look at the first draft of the initial chapters and tell me whether he thought the idea itself worthwhile and my own efforts on the right track. He was very encouraging at the time, indicating that someone needed to link the research on the historical Jesus to spirituality, and he made some very helpful suggestions. When I finished the whole manuscript, I again prevailed on him to read it and

10

comment, which he generously and graciously did. He helped me to avoid some egregious errors and to make the work more helpful. Bob Hamma of Ave Maria Press, in addition to the initial suggestion that led to this work, was also very helpful when he received the manuscript in making knowledgeable suggestions based on his own reading of recent scriptural and theological works. Kevin O'Connell, S.J., an Old Testament scholar and friend, was good enough to read the final text and to give me another theological appraisal. I am very grateful to the three of them for their help, but I have to take responsibility for the final product. Early in the project Daniel Harrington encouraged me to write to John Meier to let him know that I was relying heavily on his book and to seek comments. I am grateful to Fr. Meier for a gracious reply written while he was recovering from an illness, a reply which gave me leave to move forward (without, of course, implying endorsement for my work).

Early on I asked my friends Marika Geoghegan and Bill Russell, S.J., to read the first few chapters in rough draft. Both encouraged me and made helpful suggestions at that time, and then read the whole manuscript when I had finished the first draft and urged me to go forward with publication. My spiritual director, Anne Harvey, S.N.D., in addition to helping me to use the work to develop my own relationship with Jesus, also read the initial chapters and then the whole manuscript and urged me to publish it. I also asked Jim McDavitt, S.J., to read the manuscript. Jim and I grew up together in Worcester, Massachusetts and attended the same grammar school. When we went to different high schools we lost touch, only to find one another again in the novitiate of the New England province where Jim was a Jesuit brother novice who had entered just a couple of months before me. Now we are members of the same community. Jim read the manuscript and gave me strong encouragement. Rosalie Anderson, with her usual generosity and attention to detail, twice proofread the manuscript. Jim and Helen Milne invited me into their home for rest and relaxation. During my stay with them I put the final touches on the book. With friends like these I am a very blessed man.

The fact that I have been able to complete this book is due, in no small measure, to the staff of Jesuits and lay people who work together in the provincial offices. Without their care for detail and for people, including me, I would not have been able to write this book, nor would I have been able to do my primary job as provincial. I want to thank Rosalie Anderson, Ed Babinski, S.J., Frank Cluff, S.J., Noreen Connolly, Jack Crosby, Helen Curley, Gerte Daigle, Jack d'Anjou, S.J., Tom Gibbons, S.J., Louise Gilmore, Bob Hoey, S.J., Carole Iorio, Walter Kane, S.J., Paul Kenney, S.J., George Albert Kowalker, Jr., Jim Lafontaine, S.J., Dan Lewis, S.J., Martin MacDonnell, S.J., Norma Malave, Jim McDavitt, S.J., Tony Mejia, Kevin O'Connell, S.J., Bob Odams, and Bill Russell, S.J., for all that they do to make my job easier and enjoyable. All of the Jesuits just mentioned are part of my community, a very supportive and friendly group that also includes Al Hicks, S.J., and Ray Callahan, S.J. In this group I feel loved and supported; in addition, we enjoy one another's company and can laugh together at one another's foibles.

I dedicate the book to Jim McDavitt, S.J., who for forty years has been working at the Jesuit Seminary and

Mission Bureau to raise funds for the formation of young Jesuits and for Jesuits in foreign lands; to Ed Babinski, S.J., who for thirty-five years has been indispensable to the workings of the provincial office as secretary and factotum; and to Frank Cluff, S.J., who for thirty-four years has been working tirelessly in the treasurer's office of the New England province, twenty-two of those years as province treasurer. It gives me great consolation to dedicate this book to these wonderful Jesuit brothers who have been so helpful to me and many others.

By the way, the radiation treatments seem to have worked. There is no sign of the cancer, and my voice is back to normal.

Introduction

Just Who Is Jesus?

Recently I read three very different books. They had only one thing in common, namely, a reference to a relationship with Jesus that was striking. In her best-selling *Embraced by the Light* (written with Curtis Taylor) Betty J. Eadie dedicates the book to "the Light, my Lord and Savior Jesus Christ, to whom I owe all that I have. He is the 'staff' that I lean on; without him I would fall." The book is a rather ingenuous, unquestioning account of her near-death experience and its aftermath. Eadie may not be a critical thinker, but she obviously loves Jesus.

The American writer Reynolds Price wrote his memoir *A Whole New Life* "about a mid-life collision with cancer and paralysis, a collision I've survived for ten years and counting." In it he recounts an experience of a dream-like state in which he finds himself at the Sea of Galilee surrounded by Jesus and his apostles, is drawn by Jesus into the lake and there baptized and told his sins are forgiven. Price is quite obviously a critical thinker; he recognizes the possibility of illusion but, after sifting all the evidence, he affirms his belief that in some mysterious way this was an encounter with Jesus. He then goes on to say that the experience confirmed two old convictions.

> The first was my belief that the man Jesus, whose life and acts are reliably attested in more detail than those of Socrates or Julius Caesar, bore a mysterious relation to the creator. Whatever its nature, and my

sense is that it included some form of identity, it was a close relation which I'd long since concluded was unique in the history of human experience known to me (43).

The third book, *Paying the Price: Ignacio Ellacuria and the Murdered Jesuits of El Salvador* by Teresa Whitfield, is an exhaustive investigative report of the murder of the six Jesuits, their housekeeper, and her daughter in 1989. In it a *campesino* (a peasant worker), unsophisticated, yet full of passion, says to a Jesuit priest:

> For me Jesus is our guide. He is a leader who gave us a good example with his life. He was in favor of the poor. He wanted there to be justice, love, understanding, and peace. He spoke really strongly against those who had power and exploited the people. He persuaded the hard of heart, took the powerful down from their thrones, and all the time was in favor of the poor. He is the first person I obey and I shall follow him always, even if that means giving up my life (64).

Three very different people from widely divergent cultural backgrounds make strong affirmations about having a relationship with Jesus. These are just three examples of millions of people who consider Jesus of Nazareth their lodestar, their savior, their friend, their way to God, indeed God made flesh. To whom are all these people relating? And how did they get to know him?

It may seem that the answers to these questions are easy. After all, the gospels tell the story of his earthly life. We can read them and get some idea of who Jesus was and what he stood for. Moreover, Jesus himself promised the Holy Spirit, who would lead his followers throughout the centuries into a full knowledge of who he is. But things are not so simple after all. Many of us who relate to Jesus are aware that the gospels are not history as we have come to know it in the twentieth century. Some of us may have heard of the "quest for the historical Jesus" begun in the last century by scripture scholars. *Time* magazine (January 10, 1994) reported on the results of the "Jesus Seminar," a group of scripture scholars who have found approximately eighty-two percent of the sayings attributed to Jesus in the gospels to be inauthentic. (Raymond Brown points out, however, that their methodology is marked by the presupposition that Jesus could not have had extraordinary powers, a presupposition that runs counter to the earliest traditions about Jesus, who was remembered as a man who had precisely such powers; see *An Introduction to New Testament Christology*, 24-25.) Many may, as a result of all the publicity about the search for the historical Jesus, wonder whether we can know anything at all about him. If we cannot, is our relationship made out of whole cloth, a product of our own and others' imaginations? I want to address some of these questions in this book in order to help us to a more solid grounding in our relationship to Jesus, so that we will not be unnecessarily shaken by the claims of scholars.

Having had two very fine scripture professors when I was preparing for the priesthood, I have some sense of the fact that the gospels are not eyewitness reports of what Jesus did and said. Hence I wince when homilists speak glibly, it seems to me, of what Jesus said and did, seeming to presume that the gospels are an accurate account of the historical Jesus. But I have to admit that the shoe has often enough been on the other foot in spite of my fine professors. For example, any number of times I have referred to the story of the Syrophoenician woman to show that Jesus was a product of his own cultural prejudices and that he learned from experience.

> From there he set out and went away to the region of Tyre. He entered a house and did not want anyone to know he was there. Yet he could not escape notice, but a woman whose little daughter had an unclean spirit immediately heard about him, and she came and bowed down at his feet. Now the woman was a Gentile, of Syrophoenician origin. She begged him to cast the demon out of her daughter. He said to her, "Let the children be fed first, for it is not fair to take the children's food and throw it to the dogs." But she answered him, "Sir, even the dogs under the table eat the children's crumbs." Then he said to her, "For saying that, you may go—the demon has left your daughter." So she went home, found the child lying on the bed, and the demon gone (Mark 7:24-30).

I took the view that this story would not have been kept by the early church unless it really had happened, because it seems embarrassing to have Jesus speak so grossly to this poor woman. After all, he as much as calls her a dog because she is a Gentile, not a Jew. Imagine my chagrin when I read in the second volume of John Meier's *A Marginal Jew*: "Weighing all the pros and cons, it seems to me that the story of the Syrophoenician woman is so shot through with Christian missionary theology and concerns that creation by first-generation Christians is the more likely conclusion" (660-61). Not the first time that I have found myself mistaken. This little story, however, puts before us the question: How are we ordinary Christians to deal with the fruits of modern scriptural scholarship? More pointedly, how are we to relate to Jesus in the light of such research?

Before I go any further, I want to emphasize that any Christian can read the scriptures and gain fruit from the reading without worrying about how this or that scripture scholar interprets them. Throughout history men and women have read scripture with faith and there met the living God and Jesus, the living Son of God. For example, I believe that my relationship with Jesus was enhanced by my "mistaken" idea that the story of the Syrophoenician woman hearkened back to Jesus' own experience. I came to see that Jesus was to some extent a product of his cultural environment, just as we are, and that, as a result, he must have imbibed prejudiced notions about "foreigners" that could only be changed by experience of "foreigners" that disproved his notions. In my contemplation of the story of the Syrophoenician woman I took seriously the fact that Jesus was a real human being, and I felt closer to him, and still feel closer to him even though now I realize that the story may not reflect his actual experience. The early Christians knew Jesus to be a human being about whom such a story could be told. Moreover, they told the story to make the point that the mission of Jesus had to become more universal than just a mission to Israelites.

The words and the stories of scripture have a power to affect us profoundly whether we are aware of their origin or not. In 272 A.D. Anthony, the first desert hermit, heard the words directed to the rich young man: "Go, sell what you own, and give the money to the poor, and you will have treasure in heaven; then come, follow me" (Mark 10:21). Anthony took them as personal words to himself and immediately acted on them. More than likely he knew nothing of the history of how this text came to be put into the gospel of Mark; it would not have occurred to him to ask whether the historical Jesus actually said these words. They had a powerful effect on him, and as a result on Christendom in general, since the movement Anthony started has affected Christian spirituality and Christian religious life to the present. One can, and most Christians do, choose to believe that God spoke to Anthony through these scriptural words even though he may have known little if anything about how the scriptures came to be.

In our own day people have been known to pick up the New Testament and be swept off their feet by the power of the personality of Jesus. The Spirit of God breathes where it wills and often uses the scriptures to bring about a change of heart and direction in people who may know little about the processes by which the scriptures came to be in their present form. One need not be a scripture scholar to read the scriptures with profit and in the reading to meet the living God; nor need one be aware of the findings of scholars.

What I wonder about, however, is whether we might be better off in using the scriptures if we were more aware of the complex nature of their origins. A personal example may point us toward an answer. When the first volume of Meier's *A Marginal Jew* appeared, I picked it up and began to read it. It so happened that I was on my way to the Middle East for the first time, a trip that would take me to Amman, Beirut, and Jerusalem. John Meier's purpose is to sift all the evidence as carefully as possible in order to decide what a historian, whether a believer or not, can say about the historical Jesus. The first volume sets the stage for an investigation of the public life of Jesus by sorting through all the stories of the background and birth of Jesus. Truth to tell, we end up with the realization that we have little hard historical evidence beyond these facts: he was probably born around the year 7 or 6 B.C., grew up in Nazareth in Galilee, was a woodworker, was influenced by John the Baptist, became an itinerant preacher and baptizer, was known as a miracle worker, and died by crucifixion around 30 A.D. He was very likely able to read and write Aramaic and Hebrew and might have known some Greek.

One would think that this scholarly winnowing, which leaves precious little wheat, would have left me dry. Now the book—and its sequel—are not light reading; while well, even elegantly written, it can put one to sleep without too much trouble. And yet, at the end I was strangely moved; I felt that I was closer to Jesus than I had been before I began it. In Jordan and Israel I had a very moving sense of walking where Jesus actually walked. Now that I have finished the second volume, I have similar reactions. I have a far deeper sense of the full humanity of Jesus, of what he might have been like when he walked the roads and paths of Palestine at the beginning of our era. I believe that Jesus means more to me now than he did before I began the reading. So I presume that others, who may not have the time or the inclination or the training to make it through Meier's volumes, might be helped to a deeper relationship with Jesus by looking with me at what we can know about the historical Jesus.

A short word on the formation of the gospels and on biblical scholarship for those who might need a refresher on them. Stories about Jesus are presumed to have begun circulating even during his lifetime. After his death and resurrection his followers expected his imminent return. While waiting, they recalled stories about him and sayings of his and used these to help new converts understand who he was and is. They probably also engaged in disputes with Jewish leaders and used some of the stories and sayings in this context. It is easy to see how the original context for the stories and sayings gradually got lost as people used them for a variety of purposes.

Moreover, Jesus did not return in glory, and his followers gradually expanded beyond Jerusalem. The stories and sayings of Jesus began to be told in countries where people knew neither the geography nor the language of the land of Jesus. Another element was added to the stories and sayings as they began to be translated into other languages in other cultural and geographical contexts. Because the stories and sayings were passed on orally, they began to take on particular forms—miracle stories, parables, sermons, and so on. Units of such material (called by scholars "pericopes," literally "cut arounds") began to be used by preachers and teachers. E. P. Sanders, whom I have been following here, notes: "At some point these small units were written down and collected into larger groupings, usually on the basis of subject matter" (*The Historical Figure of Jesus*, 59). These larger groupings of pericopes were passed around in written form in the various Christian communities.

The next step seems to have been that these group-ings were put together in various places to form what scholars call "proto-gospels," "works that told a con-nected story, but not the whole story. A proto-gospel, for example, might consist of a series of pericopes dealing with conflict between Jesus and other Jews, and con-clude with his arrest, trial and execution" (*Ibid.*, 60). The writer of Mark's gospel may have used such a proto-gospel to create his conflict stories in chapters two and three. Most scholars agree that the first of our canonical gospels was put together by the writer known as Mark, perhaps as early as the 60s, and that the writers known as Matthew and Luke knew Mark's gospel and used it along with another major source which they had in common (dubbed "Q" by German scholars as short-hand for the German word *Quelle,* which means "source"), as well as other sources each of them knew separately. The gospel of John is considered to be inde-pendent of the other three (called the synoptic gospels) in the sources used. Each of the final writers of the four Gospels is considered to have written for a particular community and to have followed a particular theologi-cal line.

It is easy to see how difficult it is to get back to the historical figure of Jesus, as scholars have to sift through the various forms the gospel stories take (form criticism), the sources (source criticism), the editing done by the final writer (redaction criticism), and the community contexts in which the final writer worked (*Sitz im Leben*) to try to discover what might go back to the historical Jesus.

In his *Spiritual Exercises* Ignatius of Loyola presents a systematic method for developing a relationship with

God and for making life decisions in accordance with the truth of that relationship. The method is fueled by desires, and development in the relationship is indicated by shifts in desires. In what is known as the "Second Week" of the exercises, Ignatius assumes that the one making them has developed the desire for "an interior knowledge of Our Lord . . . that I may love him more intensely and follow him more closely" (N. 104). I presume that those who pick up this book have this desire. I am writing it with the hope that it will be a help to the attainment of this desire. In the course of the following chapters we shall be examining from a historian's perspective what we can know about the historical Jesus. However, I would counsel the reader to approach the material not with the attitude of the secular historian, but rather with the desire to have an interior knowledge of Jesus, a felt knowledge that issues in a deeper love and a desire to follow him. The scholars' labors, I believe and hope to show, can be used to help those of us who already adhere to Jesus to grow in our knowledge and love of him.

Here is my method. I believe that research on the historical Jesus need not be a threat but can be a theological and spiritual resource for us Christians. I want to demonstrate the truth of this belief. My purpose is to help readers to relate to Jesus in a personal way. Hence I engage in a work of popularization where I deliberately depend on the work of reliable scripture scholars, primarily John Meier. The book employs a method of correlation between the historical Jesus and our lives today. I will try to relate what we can know about Jesus to the experience I know best, namely my own and that of my contemporaries.

As I reflected on what I am attempting to do here, I realized that I was engaging in a kind of contemplative dialogue with Jesus. With the help of Meier's books I could get some idea of what Jesus' life might have been like. Then I asked Jesus (and myself) whether any of my own experiences might give me some more intimate knowledge of Jesus. In other words, once we have some sense of what Jesus' early life might have been like, we can engage in a sort of dialogue in which we ask Jesus whether his experience has any relation with our own. We shall see whether it works. Let it be said that the Jesus with whom we have a personal relationship is the risen Jesus, the Christ of faith. But Catholic Christianity assumes a real continuity between this person and the historical Jesus. The risen Jesus bears the marks of his historical life and death in the Palestine of the first century of our era.

The next chapter will try to situate Jesus in his social and religious culture and give a global picture of what we can know of him. In subsequent chapters I shall take up various stories about Jesus to see not only what they can tell us about the historical Jesus, but also how the gospel writers in the early church used these stories to illumine the situation of their own community. Where it can be done easily—and when I have some experience or literary reference that seems appropriate—I shall also try to show how these same biblical stories have been used by individuals and by communities of our time to get to know the living Jesus and to illumine their contemporary situations.

Jesus of 1 Nazareth

In the first volume of *A Marginal Jew* John Meier presents the evidence for the life and acts of Jesus. This evidence comes from the four gospels and other writings of the New Testament and from other writings of the era, including the history of the Jews by Josephus. Nonetheless, we must admit that the evidence does not get us very far. We can know little about Jesus of Nazareth from a strictly historical perspective. But that little may help us in our desire to know and love him better.

> *I suggest that we begin this and subsequent chapters with a prayer, similar to the desire expressed by Ignatius in the Spiritual Exercises. Perhaps something like this addressed to Jesus: "I want to know more about you so that I may love you more intensely and walk with you more closely."*

Family Background

Meier concludes from the evidence that a Jew named Yeshua (Jesus) was born around 7 or 6 B.C. He may have been born in Nazareth of Galilee, but Bethlehem of Judea is also a possibility. He certainly grew up in Nazareth, since the terms "Nazorean," "Nazarene," or "of Nazareth" were used of him almost as a second name. Now this is of considerable value for anyone who cares about Jesus. We can know where he spent most of his short life and can even visit the site or at least see pictures of the site in its present-day existence. Nazareth was a small village on a hill in southern Galilee, not far from Mount Tabor. In Jesus' day many of the houses might have been partly hollowed-out caves. Nazareth today is an Arab town; its old quarter has narrow, cramped streets. Jesus grew up in a real place whose history stretches to the present. Moreover, it was a kind of backwater town, not in the mainstream of either Jewish or Gentile life.

His mother's name was Miryam (Mary) and his putative father Yosef (Joseph). The synoptic gospels (Matthew, Mark and Luke) name four brothers of Jesus—Jacob (James), Joseph, Judah (Jude), and Simon—and mention sisters, but give no names to them. Could "brother" and "sister" mean "close relative," as some surmise? Meier decides that a historian would most likely conclude that the synoptics meant brothers and sisters, not cousins. However, other equally reputable biblical scholars say that the evidence is not as conclusive as Meier would have it. In addition, the brothers and sisters could have come from a prior marriage of Joseph (cf. Mark 6:3, where Jesus is called the son of Mary; and only after that is there mention of his brothers and sisters).

Here we see the difference between historical certainty and faith. Mary's perpetual virginity is not a historically proven fact, but it is a belief held since the early days of Christianity, as the gospels themselves attest. Those of us who believe in Mary's virginity do not do so because we have historical certitude, but because we put our trust in the ancient tradition of the church and believe that God brought about her pregnancy in some mysterious way "through the power of the Holy Spirit."

The interesting point is that the early Christians were not concerned about who these "brothers" and "sisters" of Jesus were; otherwise we would have more evidence of attempts to explain their existence. At any rate, it seems clear that Jesus did have an extended family, and undoubtedly this family had an influence on him as he grew up. We shall also see that his family was not without its tensions, much like any other family that has ever existed.

Meier notes that the immediate family circle included personal names (Miryam, Yosef, Joshua, Jacob, Judah, and so on) that refer to early Israelite history, namely, to the time of the patriarchs, the Exodus of the Israelites from Egypt, and the conquest of the Promised Land. This may indicate that the family shared in the reawakening of Jewish identity in Galilee at the time, a reawakening that yearned for the restoration of the glory days of Israel. Meier thinks it likely that Joseph, Jesus' putative father, was considered a descendant of King David; hence, the family might have shared even more deeply in these expectations, which were strong in Galilee as Jesus grew up. In other words, Jesus might well have grown up in an atmosphere of expectancy, of hope for the restoration of David's royal line. How would such an atmosphere have affected this young man, who, if the later part of his life is any indication, was deeply religious and sensitive to the call of God? As the twig is bent, so grows the tree.

Many of us who contemplate this likely bit of family history may be able to point to something similar in our own backgrounds. I grew up in a very religious family, first son of Irish immigrant parents. God was a palpable presence in our family with blessings at meals, family rosaries, frequent—even daily—Masses, and many rituals as a regular part of our life. Just the hint of thunder, for example, had my mother blessing us and the house with holy water. I have no doubt that this atmosphere played a significant part in my subsequent life. Somehow Jesus becomes less distant when I contemplate what his home life might have been like and the effect it had on his religious sensibilities. As I remember my own family life with three younger sisters, I wonder, too, whether the kind of love-hate relationships that existed among us siblings and between relatives were part of Jesus' experience. Engaging in a kind of dialogue suggested by these memories can enhance one's intimacy with Jesus.

Family Piety

Meier notes, "Jesus' family would have been imbued with an 'uncomplicated' type of Jewish piety probably widespread among the peasants of Lower Galilee" (v. II, 1039). These ordinary Galilean Jews probably had little interest in the theological disputes of the religious elite of Jerusalem. For them,

> fidelity to the Jewish religion meant fidelity to the basics spelled out in the Mosaic Law: circumcision, observance of the Sabbath, observance of kosher food laws, and pilgrimage to the Jerusalem temple, whose sacrificial ritual during the great feasts was the high point of the annual cycle of their religious life. Sur-

rounded as they were by a fair number of Gentiles and a fair amount of Hellenistic culture . . . these Galilean Jews of the countryside would cling tenaciously to the basics of their religion as "boundary symbols" reinforcing their identity (v. II, 1039-40).

We Christians often forget that Jesus was a pious Jew. We can learn something about him, I believe, by experiencing Jewish rituals. When I was a graduate student in clinical psychology, I was fortunate enough to be invited by Jewish classmates to a Seder supper celebrating Passover. I got a deep sense of how in this festive yet solemn meal, Jews experience not only their past history of deliverance but also God's saving presence now. It was a religious experience that helped me to appreciate in a small way Jesus' experience of Passover meals in his family.

I am again reminded of my own upbringing in Worcester, Massachusetts. We lived in a Catholic "ghetto," surrounded by other immigrant families. Beyond the family our identity was formed by our attachment to the parish and its Masses, novenas, and other rites. Theological niceties were not a part of our lives, just as they were probably not part of the life of Jesus. School meant going to the parish school and thus remaining apart from the surrounding dominant culture. Given that our lives were circumscribed by this Catholic culture, I am not at all sure that we were even aware that there *was* a surrounding dominant culture. We were, for the most part, insulated from that culture, perhaps as Jesus was insulated from the Hellenistic culture around him. In this "Catholic" culture I gained a sense of myself and even found a place where I could display my talents (which, at least in my early years, did not run to sports). I served as an altar boy and sang in the choir. In fact, for a rather shy if talented boy from a small neighborhood, progression from the parish and parish school to a larger Catholic high school and then to the even more heterogeneous Catholic college led to greater and greater self-confidence that might well have been aborted by an early immersion in the larger culture. Could Jesus' own growing self-confidence have been fostered by this same kind of progression? Such questions are grist for the mill of my ongoing relationship with Jesus and may give readers some hints for their own relationship with Jesus.

Education and Training

One thing, however, seems sure; Jesus did not have anything like the progression of schooling I had. He was trained as a carpenter or woodworker, presumably by Joseph, who seems to have died before Jesus' public ministry. Being trained in our father's trade is not so much a part of our culture, although my father was trained in Ireland as a blacksmith, his father's trade. My own father worked in a steel mill, and I rarely had a glimpse of him at work. I do have rather strong emotional reactions when I see a father teaching his son his trade, which might indicate a primitive desire to have had this experience myself. Jesus, it seems, did have this experience. Perhaps there is something here for conversation with him.

Jesus spoke Aramaic, probably a popular rather than a formal version, with its own peculiar characteristics. For example, in Mark's gospel he says to the daughter of Jairus, *"Talitha qum"* "Little girl, get up!"(Mark 5:41). *Qum* is the masculine form in proper

Aramaic, but in popular Aramaic it seems to have been both masculine and feminine. Thus, Jesus might well have spoken the language of the streets rather than that of the schools. He may have learned some Greek for commercial purposes or to speak with the Greek-speaking people he encountered in Galilee. He may also have known enough Hebrew to read or at least understand the scriptures read in the synagogue. He was not highly educated in the formal sense, at any rate, a fact that will make him more accessible to most Christians. When we talk with him, we do not have to use the "King's English," as it were. We can speak with him as we would speak with a friend, not as though we were in the presence of a college professor or high school grammar teacher.

Poverty

Galilean Jews of Jesus' time eked out a living. As a woodworker, Jesus would have been no different from most of his contemporaries. But he did have a trade, which gave him a living. "His socioeconomic status as well as his status as a pious Jewish layman from a pious Jewish family also assured him that modicum of honor in an honor/shame society without which ordinary people would have found existence very difficult" (v. I, 1040). In other words, Jesus' poverty need not be romanticized. It was no different than that of most of his neighbors. His situation, in fact, may have been better than most. In this he may not have been much different from many of us.

For example, I was born in 1930, a year after the beginning of the great Depression. My father worked in a steel mill as a union member. Until the years of the Second World War, work in the mill was unsteady and interrupted by strikes. As a result I grew up poor. But since all of our neighbors were in the same boat, I did not know that things could be different. Life was what it was. As children we did what we could to help out, including looking for bargains at the markets at the end of the week. I delivered papers, sold magazines, shined shoes, worked on a farm, and finally, at 13, began to work regularly in a fruit and vegetable store after school and full-time in summers. For some reason, in spite of the difference of cultures, I think that I have some feel for what Jesus experienced with regard to poverty, and it was not a type of grinding poverty that shrivels the spirit. When we talk about the poverty of Jesus, we need to remember that as a tradesman he was probably better off than the majority of the really poor of his era, and perhaps of the really poor of our world as well. As we shall see later, it could even be that Jesus' idea of God's rule or kingdom included the eradication of the evils associated with the kind of absolute poverty encountered in the great cities of our time. Perhaps Jesus intuited that God did not want such evils in his kingdom.

In another particular my growing up might have had some similarities to that of Jesus and differences from the life of many a poor child growing up in our modern inner cities. Though relatively poor, Jesus seems to have lived in an intact nuclear family and an extended family, as I did. In such a family, whatever the anxieties of making ends meet and even of the inevitable tensions bred by such anxieties, children experience a sense of security and of being cared for that is often absent today. Given a choice between affluence and such a family atmosphere, I know what I would choose, and I believe that Jesus would make the same choice. In addition, it seems Jesus experienced something that many people undergo, namely the death of his father. How did Jesus react to Joseph's death?

Culture

Galilee, especially southern Galilee, was a rather cosmopolitan territory. It was called Galilee of the Nations because so many non-Jews lived in the territory. It was a very fertile part of Palestine, studded with hamlets and villages associated with small and large cities. The Sea of Galilee was a source of fish that were exported dried to Jerusalem and even further abroad. A major trade route went through Galilee. For centuries it had been settled by people of various nationalities and religions. Only within the century before Jesus' time had it been resettled by many Jews. Thus, although the people of Galilee were looked down upon by the "sophisticated" and educated religious Jews of Jerusalem and environs, they were not necessarily "hicks." The Jews among them rubbed elbows with Greek-speaking neighbors and saw merchants from many parts of what we know as the Middle East travel through with their goods. Thus it is surmised that Jesus may have learned enough Greek to be able to carry on business with his fellow Galileans and those who passed through Galilee.

Because of the proximity of so many Gentile influences, the Galilean Jews of the lower classes held strongly to their religious traditions as a way to hold on to their distinct identity as the "chosen people." At the same time they could have developed friendships or at least neighborly relationships with non-Jews. While Jesus learned, no doubt, the distinctiveness of his own tribe and religion, he may also have learned through contact with non-Jews a toleration that was later in life expanded by further experience. Both intolerance and tolerance can develop from such closeness, as was true in my own neighborhood. Some people become friendly and even friends with "strangers," while others develop internal walls that almost nothing can breach. Another aspect of growing up in Galilee intrigues me; namely, that Galileans tended to be scorned by the sophisticates of Jerusalem. People of Irish descent like myself historically have been scorned as of low cultural attainment. I confess to having felt some of this in my younger days when I first went to college. It did my heart good to realize the love of learning that is ingrained in the Irish culture and the centuries of artistic and literary attainments of my people. Perhaps Jesus developed the same kind of pride in what his people had achieved in learning and culture.

During his ministry Jesus used parables to get across his message. His parables used images from daily life in the villages and rural areas of Galilee: farming in hill country (Mark 4:4-7), sheep herding (Matt 18:12-14), patched cloaks (Matt 9:16), lilies of the field (Matt 6:28), lamps in a one-room home (Matt 5:15). If we contemplate his parables, we find out a good deal about Jesus. We see that he knows the ordinary life of the poor, that he has a vivid and creative imagination, that he likes to jolt people in order to impress on them his view of God and of God's kingdom. For example, even we can be shocked by the parable of the owner of the vineyard who pays those who have only worked one hour the same wage as he pays those who have worked the whole day (Matt 20:1-16). Contemplation of the parables of Jesus is a good way to get to know what experiences made a deep impression on Jesus and what he cared about.

Jesus the Celibate

There is little else remarkable that we know about Jesus prior to the beginning of his public life. One thing that did make him atypical among his contemporaries, Meier notes, is the fact that he never married. This was a highly unusual choice among young men of his time. He would have been about thirty-four years old when he forsook Nazareth and his relatively settled life as a woodworker. Not to have been married by that time indicates a deliberate choice, and one that would have gone against the customs of his family, friends, and culture. Why would he have made this choice? A good question, the answer to which can only be speculative. However, the question can enter into the dialogue with Jesus. Could it be that long before he finally broke from his family and his way of life he already had stirrings of the sense of the imminent coming of God's kingdom that made it impossible for him to contemplate marriage and family life? As we shall see in a later chapter, his public ministry was consumed with a sense of urgency about the coming of God's kingdom; it may be that this urgency had already begun to stir in him much earlier in his life.

Here my own experience cannot be a guide. Becoming a celibate religious or priest was not unusual in the culture in which I grew up. In fact, in those days families felt honored if one of their children entered a religious congregation or seminary. Perhaps those who feel called to a celibate life in these days, when entrance into a religious congregation is relatively rare and priestly celibacy is under attack, have a deeper understanding of Jesus' unusual choice. At any rate, the fact that Jesus did make this unusual choice can give us an opening for engaging in dialogue with him about celibacy and about sexuality. Even though he chose to be a celibate, he remained a sexual human being and had to deal creatively with the erotic and sexual aspects of his being. We can, therefore, discuss with him our own erotic and sexual desires, fantasies, hopes, and fears and hope not only for understanding but also for a sense of how he dealt with his sexuality.

Leaving Home

Jesus could have stayed in Nazareth all his life. Obviously he made a different choice. Now we must turn to his public life and what we can know of it from the sources available to us. As Meier says:

> Somewhere around 28 A.D., Jesus broke with his honorable though modest socioeconomic status, his settled life in Nazareth, and his close family ties to undertake the unusual role of an itinerant celibate layman proclaiming the imminent arrival of the kingdom of God. Being about thirty-four years old at the time he began his ministry, Jesus would have already seemed unusual or socially marginal in the eyes of his fellow Jews by his conscious choice of a celibate state. He now made himself even more unusual or marginal by his consciously chosen ministry of an itinerant prophet of the end time. He had

obviously lost the honor accruing to his former state of life. Whether he gained a new kind of honor in the eyes of at least some Jews depended on whether or not his audience believed him (v. II, 1040-41).

Jesus and 2
John the Baptist

What motivated Jesus to take the decisive step to enter public life when he did history cannot say. But history can say that the figure of another marginal Jew, John, known as the Baptizer, played a very significant role in his life at this time. In this chapter I want to look at that role. We want to get to know Jesus better in order to be better friends and disciples of his.

We begin, as usual, with the desire that might be addressed to Jesus in words such as these: "I want to know more about you so that I may love you more intensely and walk with you more closely."

John the Baptist

Somewhere around 28 A.D. an ascetic prophet named John appeared "in the desert," that is, in the lower Jordan valley. There he proclaimed in powerful sermons the imminent coming of God's fiery judgment on all of Israel. As far as we know, John did not cite scripture or engage in lengthy arguments to justify his claims. He spoke with authority and power of the sins of the Israelites and called them to repentance in order to save themselves from the wrath that would surely come. In addition, he demanded that they receive baptism from him in the Jordan River as a condition and sign of their repentance. Because the judgment was upon them, this baptism was a once-and-for-all event. John's tone and words were stark and threatening, even to those who approached him for baptism. "You brood of vipers! Who warned you to flee from the wrath to come? Bear fruits worthy of repentance. . . . Even now the ax is lying at the root of the trees; every tree therefore that does not bear good fruit is cut down and thrown into the fire" (Luke 3:7-9). It would not be easy to escape the fiery judgment. While making himself and his baptism central to salvation, John also spoke mysteriously of a "stronger one" who would come after him and who would baptize with the Holy Spirit (Luke 3:16).

From the point of view of the historian it is unclear whether by the "stronger one" (who for the evangelists is Jesus) John meant God, Michael the archangel, Elijah, Elisha, or another of the dead prophets, a royal or priestly messiah, a final prophet, or Jesus. Meier indicates that it might have been unclear to John himself. At any rate, John's message was paradoxical: on the one hand, he tied salvation from the imminent fiery judgment of God to his own person, preaching and baptism; on the other hand, in all humility he pointed to another "stronger one" with a superior baptism. But the message John delivered was urgent; the time for repentance was *now*, because judgment was hanging over the Israelites. Moreover, the message was dire: "The spirit will be poured out in the future only on those repentant Israelites on whom John pours out his water now; for all others there waits only fire" (v. II, 40).

Many Jews went out to the Jordan to receive the saving baptism of John. They, too, felt that the times were out of joint and that judgment was imminent. For them, John was at least a prophet, if not *the* prophet of the end time. Indeed, it may have been their tendency to see him as *the* prophet that led John to speak of the "stronger one." To say this is to assume that while John was sure of his call to preach an imminent judgment, he was also sure that he himself was not the final prophet.

Jesus, the Possible Disciple of John

It is likely that word of this charismatic figure reached Jesus in Nazareth. Biblical scholars agree that Jesus was baptized by John in the Jordan and that this event marked the break with his past life in Nazareth. Moreover, as Meier points out, Jesus' public ministry as we know it makes no sense without the influence of John the Baptist. Could it be that the news about John was the final catalyst that stirred Jesus to leave Nazareth to see for himself, that what Jesus heard of John's message somehow resonated with what was going on in his own spirit? This kind of question might lead to a fruitful conversation with Jesus. It builds on what is known with some certitude about the historical Jesus and allows us to let the Lord use our imaginations to develop a more intimate relationship with Jesus.

The kind of prayer suggested here is what is called "contemplation" in the *Spiritual Exercises* of Ignatius of Loyola. Persons contemplating a gospel text let it touch their imagination in the same way that imaginative literature does. They imagine themselves present to the scene depicted: they see the people, listen to what they are saying, feel what they are feeling. Ignatius, for example, suggests that retreatants imagine themselves present on the road to Bethlehem with Mary and Joseph and at the stable as Jesus is born. The gospels are written to stir our imaginations so that we might believe. (For more on this kind of prayer see my book *What Do I Want in Prayer?*, chapter 9.) For purposes of this book, however, instead of taking the gospel text as the starting point, I suggest starting with what we can know with some certitude about the historical Jesus and letting that knowledge stir our imaginations.

People who have themselves been stirred in their youth to seek out a charismatic figure by hearing reports about him or her or who have heard stories of such stirrings will have something to go on as they enter into this kind of imaginative prayer. What was the significance for Jesus of being baptized by John? Meier writes:

> By doing this Jesus acknowledged John's charismatic authority as an eschatological prophet [a prophet of the end time], accepted his message of imminent fiery judgment on a sinful Israel, submitted to his baptism as a seal of his resolve to change his life and as a pledge of salvation as part of a purified Israel, on whom God (through some agent?) would pour out the holy spirit on the last day. All this tells us something of Jesus' view of John (v. II, 116).

Moreover, while Jesus added some significant new elements to the teaching of John, throughout his public ministry he stood for what John the Baptist did. Like John, Jesus proclaimed an imminent coming of God's kingdom in judgment; demanded an inner change of heart to be ready for this coming; gathered around himself disciples, including an inner circle; made people's

41

WHO DO YOU SAY I AM?

stance toward him a touchstone of salvation; may have conferred baptism on those who were ready to accept him and his message; and engaged in an itinerant ministry as a celibate. John was, it seems, Jesus' mentor. It cannot be proven, but Meier believes it likely that Jesus was for a time after his baptism a disciple of John. It makes Jesus more human and approachable to realize that he, like us, came under the influence of a mentor.

Moreover, Jesus remained respectful of John and, apparently, cognizant of what he owed to him. Meier argues that much of the praise of John in Matthew 11: 7-11 can probably be attributed to the historical Jesus.

> "What did you go out into the wilderness to look at? A reed shaken by the wind? What then did you go out to see? Someone dressed in soft robes? Look, those who wear soft robes are in royal palaces. What then did you go out to see? A prophet? Yes, I tell you, and more than a prophet. . . . Truly I tell you, among those born of women no one has arisen greater than John the Baptist; yet the least in the kingdom of heaven is greater than he."

This text reflects some of the scenery of the lower Jordan (reeds shaking in the wind), perhaps refers in an oblique way to Herod Antipas, to whom John would not bend (soft robes in royal palaces), and indicates the kind of lively repartee and irony Jesus can use to make a point. Moreover, there is an indication in the last verse that Jesus has become conscious that with his ministry something new has entered history; while John had no equal in the old dispensation, in this new age anyone who accepts Jesus is "greater than" John.

There is something worth pondering here. Jesus is aware that he has brought something new into the equation announced by John. The kingdom of God announced by Jesus is a new "field of force," as Meier puts it. Jesus has gone beyond his mentor. But unlike so many who break from their mentors, Jesus does not have to denigrate John in order to establish himself. Here is fruit for dialogue with Jesus. If you are like me, for example, you know how easy it is to build yourself up at the expense of your predecessor in a job. What kind of a person is this Jesus who has so much self-confidence, or confidence in God, that he can recognize both his debt to John and his differences from him while at the same time praising him to the skies?

Jesus Beyond John

While Jesus was and remained indebted to John for both his teaching and his style of ministry, there were differences between them in both. Meier believes that the text in Matthew's gospel just prior to the one we have cited also reflects a historical event, namely, John's question about the meaning of the ministry of Jesus about which he had been hearing. John expected that God's fiery judgment would come in his lifetime, and that it would be a harsh judgment. But it had not yet come. Moreover, he had heard of the ministry of this former disciple of his, whose message, while in many ways similar to his own, diverged from it in crucial ways. John's was a harsh message, and John neither claimed to be nor was considered a miracle worker. While Jesus could thunder with the best of them (see Matt 11:21ff: "Woe to you, Chorazin! Woe to you, Bethsaida"), still he emphasized the good news of God's rule and indicated that that rule was already powerfully at work in his own healings and exorcisms and in his table fellowship with sinners and tax collectors. In a sense Jesus' star was rising even while John continued his ministry in the Jordan valley. Once his ministry was curtailed by his imprisonment, John must have begun to wonder what was happening. John, like Jesus, seems to have been a large-hearted man; he did not seek to denigrate Jesus' achievements. Rather, Meier conjectures, John was faced with a serious question, and so he sent disciples to ask Jesus: "Are you the one who is to come, or are we to wait for another?"

Jesus' response is indirect and does not make any messianic claims. He just tells them what is being said about him on all sides with an oblique reference to a prophecy of Isaiah 35, and in doing so focuses on those aspects of his ministry which diverge most from the ministry of John. "Go and tell John what you hear and see: the blind receive their sight, the lame walk, the lepers are cleansed, the deaf hear, the dead are raised, and the poor have good news brought to them" (Matt 11:2-5). Jesus tells John that God's coming will be a joyful one, bringing good news and healing, a far cry from the coming prophesied by John. The final verse of this section may be an expression of hope that John would not be scandalized by Jesus: "And blessed is anyone who takes no offense at me" (v. 6). Meier speculates that this verse may contain an implicit threat aimed at the Baptist, as though Jesus were saying, "If you are scandalized at me, perhaps you will not be blessed."

It is rather refreshing to consider that Jesus had to come to terms with going beyond his mentor and perhaps with scandalizing him by the content of his message. What was it like for Jesus to realize that he had to preach a message different from that of John? Did he wonder how John would react? Did he have to over-come any doubts about his different message? Certain-ly there is matter for dialogue with Jesus here. Moreover, we can find in both of these men a combina-tion of qualities that so often meet like oil and water, namely, self-assurance and humble self-effacement.

The very next section of Matthew's gospel has an-other episode that Meier and many other exegetes con-sider a parable spoken by Jesus. Here, too, we learn something about Jesus' relation to John and about the different ways the two men were judged in their own time.

> "But to what will I compare this generation? It is like children sitting in the marketplaces and calling to one another, 'We played the flute for you, and you did not dance; we wailed, and you did not mourn.' For John came neither eating nor drinking, and they say, 'He has a demon'; the Son of Man came eating and drinking, and they say, 'Look, a glutton and a drunkard, a friend of tax collectors and sinners!'" (Matt 11:16-19).

Notice that Jesus has paid attention to children at some kind of game and seems to have gotten a kick out of it. It is not clear what the game is, but at the least he has noticed it and seen how funny children can be when they get into a stalemate in a game. The most likely scenario is that one group of children tried to get another to engage in play, first one way, then another, but the second group refused to join. It says something about Jesus that he would have paid attention to these children at play and that he would have been amused by them. Perhaps this insight may help you in relating with Jesus.

Now notice how Jesus uses what he has seen to drive home a telling point that he hopes will startle his hearers. Jesus likens the present generation to the second group of children. John came with an ascetic life style, a stern mien, and a warning, and he was turned away because he was so severe; Jesus presents a contrasting picture, but is turned away as well, because of his "free" style. In this contrast Jesus does not denigrate John's style; he is noting matters of fact. John was an ascetic; Jesus was not. This was accepted by Jesus and apparently so well known as to be a matter for comment by many and rejection by some. Those who were rejecting his message latched onto his lifestyle to accuse him of being a glutton and a drunkard. Neither Jesus nor the gospel writers claim that Jesus lived an ascetic lifestyle. He did indeed enjoy eating food and drinking wine. In a footnote Meier notes: "Palestinian people of poor or moderate means would tend to identify regular drinking of wine—so regular that the person in question became known for it in public—with both affluence and indulgence" (v. II, 211). Just these few facts could lead to a fruitful conversation with Jesus about his lifestyle and about our own. At the least we see here that Jesus marched to a different drummer than John in terms of lifestyle, yet Jesus does not need to exalt his own way of being at the expense of John's.

A closer look at the end of the passage yields even more fruit for our desire to know Jesus more intimately in order to love him more and to follow him more closely. It is said of Jesus, as another reason to reject his message, that he is "a friend of tax collectors and sinners." Tax collectors were disliked, at least in Galilee, not so much because they collected taxes for the hated

Romans and thus could be considered traitors, but because they were considered dishonest, men who charged more than was required and kept the extra for themselves. And "sinners" were not the simple folk of the land who had neither the time nor the inclination to know and follow all the niceties of the Law (in other words, the "likes of us"), but rather people who were actually irreligious. They were, says Sanders (*The Historical Figure of Jesus*), the "wicked" of Psalm 10:

> For the wicked boast of the desires of their heart,
> those greedy for gain curse and renounce the LORD.
> In the pride of their countenance the wicked say,
>   "God will not seek it out";
> all their thoughts are, "There is no God" (Ps 10:3-4).

Meier notes:

> Sinners were those who intentionally rejected the commandments of the God of Israel, as these commandments were understood by Jews in general, not just by an elite group of puritans. Jesus' table fellowship was therefore seriously offensive to many Jews, not just to . . . Pharisees. He insisted on entering into intimate relationship not only with dishonest Jews who robbed their fellows (the tax collectors) but also with those Jews who, for all practical purposes, had thumbed their noses at the covenant and commandments of God. It was to these wicked that Jesus dared to offer forgiveness and a place in the kingdom of God, without apparently making it a prior condition that they go through the usual process of reintegration into Jewish religious society: prayers of repentance, restitution of ill-gotten goods or recompense for harm committed, temple sacrifice, and commitment to following the Mosaic Law. His bon vivant

existence with robbers and sinners was therefore
something much more scandalous and ominous than
a mere matter of breaking purity rules dear to the . . .
Pharisees (v. II, 149).

It is one of the strongest arguments for the historical
authenticity of much of this passage (Matt 11:16-19)
that it was kept by the early church in spite of what it
said about Jesus. To bring the point home to ourselves,
it seems that we have to imagine Jesus sitting down for
food and drink with petty crooks who, for example,
steal checks from the mail or prey on the poor, or with
men and women born Catholic who have no regard for
the church and its practices and do not mind letting us
know it. Here we have matter indeed for conversation
with Jesus as we continue to try to get to know him. It is
not the image we ordinarily have of Jesus. We shall return to his table fellowship with tax collectors and sinners later when we take up some of the reasons why
Jesus became so hated that he was crucified.

Jesus and John in the Early Church

I believe that I have said enough to give the reader a
flavor of the actual relationship of Jesus and John inso-
far as this can be discovered by historical scholarship. It
might be of some interest to see how the early church
approached this relationship. There is evidence that
John's influence lived on after his death. There are two
stories in Acts that show that John's movement was
alive at least in Alexandria and Ephesus (Acts 18:24-25;
19:1-3). Scholars believe that the early church had a
somewhat difficult dilemma; namely, to acknowledge
the importance of John and at the same time to indicate
the superiority of Jesus. Luke's gospel, for example, in

the infancy narratives makes John a relative of Jesus and in the stories themselves indicates that from the womb John acknowledged the superiority of Jesus. Another example: Matthew's gospel introduces a dialogue between Jesus and John at the time of Jesus' baptism. When Jesus approaches John for baptism, John protests: "I need to be baptized by you, and do you come to me?" Jesus replies: "Let it be so now; for it is proper for us in this way to fulfill all righteousness." Only then does John consent (Matt 3:14-15). Behind the introduction of this dialogue interpreters read some embarrassment among Christians that Jesus submitted to John's baptism and in so doing admitted to being, at the least, part of a sinful people. All the gospels are careful to distinguish Jesus from John and to make sure that the reader will recognize the distinction.

In addition, the gospels use the stories of John and Jesus to speak to their own actual community situations. One example seems to occur in Matthew's gospel. In his translation and commentary on Matthew, Daniel Harrington writes:

> The Pharisees were most likely the chief rivals of Matthew and his community after the destruction of Jerusalem and its temple in A.D. 70. It is also likely that Matthew has sharpened and even exaggerated the negative portrayal of the Pharisees during Jesus' time in light of his experience with them after A.D. 70 *(The Gospel of Matthew, 57).*

Where Luke's gospel has John calling the crowds who come for baptism "You brood of vipers!" (Luke 3:7), Matthew makes the Pharisees and Sadducees the object of this tirade (Matt 3:7ff). We should not be surprised at this. Preachers throughout history have taken

49

stories of Jesus and used them to illuminate the problems faced by their communities. The gospels are not historical documents such as we are used to. They work with the materials gathered together in various sources to provide the people of their time an opportunity to know Jesus—to believe in him—in order to love him and follow him.

The story of John's testimony to Jesus in John's gospel will give us an opportunity to see how the relationship between Jesus and John still plays itself out in our day. John's disciples have come to him to ask him about Jesus.

> John answered, "No one can receive anything except what has been given from heaven. You yourselves are my witnesses that I said, 'I am not the Messiah, but I have been sent ahead of him.' He who has the bride is the bridegroom. The friend of the bridegroom, who stands and hears him, rejoices greatly at the bridegroom's voice. For this reason my joy has been fulfilled. He must increase, but I must decrease" (John 3:27-30).

Here again we see how the gospel writer has worked the material to underline the superiority of Jesus. Many a time when I have contemplated this scene I have asked to be given the grace received by John, that is, to want only one thing, that Jesus be better known no matter what happens to me. That I still have a long way to go is clear whenever I examine my state of consciousness and realize how much it matters what people think of me, how often, even when I preach or write, I think of the impact I am making and not of Jesus and his message. Nonetheless, the prayer of desire I make is, I believe, authentic, and I remain hopeful that eventually the Lord will burn away my self-centeredness as the story indicates he did with John.

The Relationship as Seen Today

The modern Japanese novelist Shusaku Endo has written an imaginative life of Jesus. He takes the gospel stories and lets his creative imagination work with the material about Jesus and John. In *A Life of Jesus* he takes it for granted that Jesus had a different conception of God than John had. The question is: How did he come to this new idea of God? Endo imagines that Jesus learned something new about God when he went out into the desert for forty days. There, according to Endo's imaginative re-creation, he learned that the seemingly harsh and demanding God of John is really a God of love, a God who can be called Abba, "my own dear Father." The novelist has approached the gospel material contemplatively and has had an insight into Jesus that helps him (and his readers) to know Jesus better. In this chapter I have suggested that we use our imaginations in a similar way in order to let Jesus reveal to us some of what he felt as he came under the influence of John and later moved beyond him.

The Message 3 of Jesus: The Kingdom of God

In the last chapter we mentioned Jesus' preaching of the kingdom of God. If there is one thing that can be said with certainty about Jesus' message, it is that he made the concept or symbol "kingdom of God" central to his teaching. If we want to know the historical Jesus better, we must come to terms with the meaning for him of this elusive and allusive term.

As we begin this chapter, let us once again express our desire: "I want to know more about you so that I may love you more intensely and walk with you more closely."

Sayings About the Kingdom

Let me first indicate some of the sayings of Jesus about the kingdom of God that are deemed to derive from his own teaching. In citing these texts I am not indicating that the whole saying is verbatim from Jesus, only that the core of the saying seems to derive from him. Nor am I saying that only these sayings can be traced to the historical Jesus.

In the only prayer Jesus is said to have taught his disciples he tells them to pray, "Your kingdom come"

(Matt 6:10). While marveling at the faith of the centurion Jesus says, "I tell you, many will come from east and west and will eat with Abraham and Isaac and Jacob in the kingdom of heaven, while the heirs of the kingdom will be thrown into outer darkness, where there will be weeping and gnashing of teeth" (Matt 8:11-12). In the beatitudes Jesus says, "Blessed are you who are poor, for yours is the kingdom of God" (Luke 6:20). In a dispute with his enemies Jesus says, "But if it is by the finger of God that I cast out the demons, then the kingdom of God has come to you" (Luke 11:20). "Once Jesus was asked by the Pharisees when the kingdom of God was coming, and he answered, 'The kingdom of God is not coming with things that can be observed; nor will they say, 'Look, here it is! or There it is! For, in fact, the kingdom of God is among you'" (Luke 17:20-21). In addition, there are also the "kingdom parables" in which the kingdom of God is compared to yeast, a mustard seed, a lost pearl, and so on. It seems clear that this symbol meant a great deal to Jesus.

Meaning of the Kingdom of God

But what did Jesus mean by the kingdom of God? It is quite clear that Jesus was not referring to a territorial kingdom, a religious political entity. Sanders states: "The only thing that Jesus ever asks people to do is to live right. In none of the material does he urge them to build an alternative society that will be the kingdom of God" (*The Historical Figure of Jesus*, 178).

The Lord's Prayer

Let us approach an answer through the Lord's Prayer. Meier concludes that the core of the prayer as taught by Jesus ran: "Father, hallowed be your name.

Your Kingdom come. Our daily bread give us today. And forgive us our debts as we forgive our debtors. And do not lead us to the test." "Father" translates Abba, Jesus' unique and striking way of addressing God. Meier translates it as "My own dear father" and says of the petitions that follow: "The surprisingly direct and short petitions are meant to reproduce the trusting and unaffected attitude of a child dependent on an all-powerful and loving father" (v. II, 294). Jesus' experience of God as "my own dear Father" could be the focus of a period of prayer, indeed, of many periods of prayer. Obviously Jesus' experience was different from the experience of John the Baptist, who also prayed that God come in power to rule. Certainly Jesus knew God as transcendent Mystery itself, as the awesome One before whom all that is created is as nothing. Jesus never repudiates the God of the Hebrew scriptures or of John the Baptist. At the same time Jesus can speak with tenderness of this God as "my own dear Father." Most of us, I believe, find it hard to hold together these two images of God in a creative tension. We tend to one or the other side of the equation: holding an image either of an implacable, all-powerful, demanding God or of a sweet, old, grandfather God. We might want to ask Jesus to help us to have his image of God.

Now we return to the Lord's Prayer and what it teaches about Jesus' image of the kingdom of God. Having instructed the disciples to address God in this familiar way, Jesus then tells them to pray: "Hallowed be your name. Your kingdom come." These petitions ask God to make the divine name holy, that is, to glorify God's name, and to have the kingdom come. In the original Aramaic these two petitions would have had a parallel structure; hence, it is argued, the two petitions say something about God's action.

God's name refers to God as revealed. Thus Jesus prays that God be revealed, making himself holy or glorified, showing God as who God really is. Meier refers us to the words of God in the prophet Ezekiel:

> It is not for your sake, O house of Israel, that I am about to act, but for the sake of my holy name, which you have profaned among the nations to which you came. I will sanctify [hallow] my great name, which has been profaned among the nations, and which you have profaned among them; and the nations shall know that I am the Lord, says the Lord, when through you I display my holiness before their eyes (Ezek 36:22-24).

God promises to make the name holy by intervening in the history of the chosen people, by bringing them back from exile, forgiving them, and giving them a new heart. Thus when Jesus prayed "Hallowed be your name," he was asking for God's self-revelation in a saving way.

In the same fashion God's kingdom refers to God as ruling. Theologian Roger Haight writes: "The reign of God is God's will being done" (*Discovery*, No. 5, December 15, 1994). Thus Jesus prays that God come as ruler, as one whose will is carried out. In a sense he is asking for the same thing as when he prayed "hallowed be your name." He asks that God come in power to save and restore the chosen people. Given the biblical background, we can say that Jesus is asking God to bring about the promise of a new and everlasting covenant, in which all Israel acknowledges God as the only One and lives according to God's desires.

In short, when Jesus prays that God's kingdom come, he is simply expressing in a more abstract phrase the eschatological hope of the latter part of the OT [Old Testament] and the pseudepigrapha [writings not considered part of the canonical OT] that God would come on the last day to save and restore his people Israel (Meier, v. II, 299).

Jesus prays and instructs his disciples to pray for the final victory of God, for what God intends for humanity, indeed, for the world. This final victory is what Jesus preaches, not himself. In other words, God and God's initiative are key for Jesus, not what he himself says or does.

This may be a good time to say something about the word *eschatology* and its adjective *eschatological*. Eschatology refers to the end times (*eschata* being the Greek word for "last things"). Sanders notes that "Jesus did not expect the end of the world in the sense of the destruction of the cosmos. He expected a divine, transforming miracle" along the lines of God's earlier interventions into the history of the chosen people. "In the future, Jesus thought that God would act even more decisively: he would create an ideal world. He would restore the twelve tribes of Israel, and peace and justice would prevail" (*The Historical Figure of Jesus*, 183-84).

The Kingdom Is Not Yet Present

Obviously, if Jesus prays for the rule of God to come, it is not yet here. The world as Jesus knows it is not entirely under the rule of God. For Jesus, it seems, sickness, blindness, possession of individuals by Satan, injustice, poverty, blasphemy, and sinfulness are all signs that God does not yet fully rule. Jesus wants God to rule. As we shall see, he seems to have believed that his healings and exorcisms were signs that God's rule was, in some sense, already present. At the same time, even though sickness, blindness, and other evils must be rooted out for God to rule, God's rule is still not wholly a worldly reality; it has a transcendent dimension to it. "I tell you, many will come from east and west and will eat with Abraham and Isaac and Jacob in the kingdom of heaven, while the heirs of the kingdom will be thrown into outer darkness, where there will be weeping and gnashing of teeth" (Matt 8:11-12). God's rule will not only transcend the limitations of time and place and death but also the limitations of tribal belonging; at least some Gentiles will sit down at the banquet in the definitive rule of God. Moreover, it seems that Jesus himself looked forward to this transcendent dimension. He is recorded as saying at the Last Supper: "Truly I tell you, I will never again drink of the fruit of the vine until that day when I drink it new in the kingdom of God" (Mark 14:25). Meier believes this saying to be from Jesus himself and to have been connected with the Last Supper. Sensing that death is near, Jesus still believes that his cause is God's cause and that God will yet vindicate him, will yet rule and include Jesus in the heavenly banquet that Jesus associates with God's rule.

In addition, Jesus seems to have believed that God's definitive rule was imminent, though not yet present. There is an urgency to his preaching, an urgency reminiscent of the preaching of John the Baptist. We have become so used to praying "your kingdom come" that we have lost the sense of urgency that the words had for the historical Jesus, and even for the early church.

Jesus seems to believe that the coming of God's rule is connected with his life and work, although it is not evident that he ever gave a clear indication of when God's rule would arrive.

Still, we have to recognize that the early Christians had a very difficult time when the coming of the kingdom, Jesus' second coming, was delayed, and more and more of the first Christians died. This problem challenged Paul in his First Letter to the Thessalonians. Sanders argues that the pieces of evidence showing that the early Christians had to revise their expectations about the triumphal coming of God's kingdom again and again can best be explained "if we think that Jesus himself told his followers that the Son of Man would come while they still lived. The fact that this expectation was difficult for Christians in the first century helps prove that Jesus held it himself. We also note that Christianity survived this early discovery that Jesus had made a mistake very well" (*The Historical Figure of Jesus*, 180).

Raymond Brown is less sure than Sanders that Jesus told his followers that the Son of Man would come while they still lived, but he does indicate that the evidence argues for a certain vagueness in Jesus about when the end would come. After showing that theological attempts to explain away statements attributed to Jesus about the final coming go to rather desperate lengths, Brown asks, "Is it inconceivable that, since Jesus did not know when God would bring about the final victory of the kingdom, he tended to think that it would occur soon and spoke accordingly?" (*An Introduction to New Testament Christology*, 58). Catholic Christians proclaim that Jesus was fully human as well as

God. To be fully human means not to know the future; it is no imperfection to be ignorant of the future. In the fourth eucharistic prayer the priest prays, "He was conceived through the power of the Holy Spirit, and born of the Virgin Mary like us in all things but sin." All that we need to affirm of Jesus is that as a human being he was sinless.

Recently I was contemplating the transfiguration at a time when I was anxious about the future. It came to me that life as a human being means to live as if in the cloud that came over Jesus and the disciples in that scene. In the Hebrew Scriptures God's presence is signified by a cloud. In the image we are all enveloped in the cloud that is God present and acting in our world. We must live without knowing the future, trusting in God to guide us. Jesus had to live the same way, trusting in God to bring about the kingdom. Admittedly, it was difficult for early Christians, as it is for many of us, to admit that Jesus was mistaken or at least in the dark about the imminence of God's coming rule. But even for the one whom Christians proclaim as the Son of God, the price of being fully human, perhaps, is to be unable to predict the future accurately. There is food for thought here and for conversation with Jesus.

A Reflection on Jesus

Let's pause here to consider what we have learned about Jesus by this study of his preoccupation with God's rule. Jesus was obsessed with God and God's rule. He was not a political reformer or an anti-Roman Jewish leader. Only God can bring about God's rule, that is, what God intends. Moreover, Jesus was not a religious functionary, someone for whom carrying on the religious rituals of his religion defined his identity. He was single-mindedly focused on God, and he had a profound sense of what God wants of humanity and of creation. We might say that he was obsessed with God's project. He seems to have sensed that his time and he himself were pivotal in the history of God's people, perhaps in the history of creation. God was about to do something definitive to bring about God's rule in the world, and Jesus could do no other than to preach in season and out, in one way and another: "The time is fulfilled, and the kingdom of God has come near" (Mark 1:15).

At the same time, Jesus was no religious fanatic, someone who had to sweep up others into his orbit by hook or by crook in order to achieve what he believed God wanted. He does not seem to have whipped up crowds to follow him. According to John's gospel, Jesus tried to avoid the kind of mass hysteria that would have pushed people to make him a political or religious leader: "When Jesus realized that they were about to come and take him by force to make him king, he withdrew again to the mountain by himself" (John 6: 15; see also Mark 1:35-37).

Have you ever met a person like this? Would you like to get to know Jesus better, to get to know what made him tick? Would you want to have the same kind of single-minded focus on God that he had? Even if the answer to the last question is equivocal, still we do have grist for the mill of our conversations with Jesus.

In another work (*Spiritual Direction and The Encounter with God*) I have referred to the philosophy of John Macmurray in speaking of Jesus' concept of the kingdom of God. Macmurray's philosophy of the person focuses on the actions of persons. Actions are governed by intentions. I act in order to accomplish something. At the end of his Gifford lectures (*The Form of the Personal*) Macmurray comes to the idea of the universe as the one action of God, governed by one intention. The universe is, thus, God's freely chosen project. And God intends something with this one action that is the universe. I have come to believe that what Jesus intends with the symbol of the kingdom of God can be understood as the universe under God's rule or intention. God's one action includes all the events that make up the universe and all the actions of free beings in history, some of which are in harmony with God's one action and intention, some of which are not. But no matter what human beings do, whether they act in tune with God's intention or not, God continually is acting to bring about the universe, God's one action. Whether we know it or not, we are engaged in this one action of God, and we are being drawn by God to conform our actions with this one action. To revert to an earlier image, the universe as God's one action is the cloud in the midst of which each of us acts.

Now Jesus, as a first-century Palestinian woodworker, would not have had a clue about modern philosophy or perhaps even the philosophy of his own time. He would never have used the kind of language I take from Macmurray. Nonetheless, he intuited that God is acting in history all the time and believed that God was acting especially strongly in his time because it was the "time of fulfillment." He could do no other than to give himself wholeheartedly to God's project and to try to get his compatriots to do the same. Moreover, he seems to have believed that the forces arrayed against God were also very active and that no one could remain on the sidelines in this epic battle. "Whoever is not against us is for us" (Mark 9:40). Meier puts it this way:

> It is important to realize that, in the view of Jesus . . . human beings were not basically neutral territories that might be influenced by divine or demonic forces now and then. . . . Human existence was seen as a battlefield dominated by one or the other supernatural force, God or Satan (alias Belial or the devil). A human being might have a part in choosing which "field of force" would dominate his or her life, i.e., which force he or she would choose to side with. But no human being was free to choose simply to be free of these supernatural forces. One was dominated by either one or the other, and to pass from one was necessarily to pass into the control of the other. At least over the long term, one could not maintain a neutral stance vis-a-vis God and Satan (v. II, 415).

Since the time of Jesus, Christian religious geniuses—who have believed in Jesus as far more than just a religious genius, by the way—have also become aware of this epic battle. In his own very turbulent time Ignatius of Loyola, who lived at the end of the medieval synthesis and the beginning of the modern world, came to believe that the human heart was a battleground between God and the evil one, between good spirits and evil spirits, and that it was necessary to discern these different spirits and ask to be put under the influence of the good spirits. It is possible that the urgency of the coming of God's rule strikes religious geniuses in times of great turmoil, such as in Jesus' time and the time of Ignatius. If that is so, then our time could certainly qualify, especially at the end of the second millennium, as a time of heightened awareness of how much the times are out of joint, far from what God intends, and hence ripe for a new and perhaps final coming of God to rule. I engage in this digression from the search for the historical Jesus to help the reader put what we have seen of Jesus in a context that might help us to get a feel for Jesus and his message.

The Kingdom as the Reversal of Values

In the Hebrew scriptures and for Jesus, God's rule meant a reversal of the ills of people and of society. God as the just king will take care of widows and orphans and the poor, and will right the injustices that seem endemic to any political arrangement that does not acknowledge God and God's intention as sovereign not only in word but especially in deed. The beatitudes of Jesus (Matt 5:1-11; Luke 6:20-23) announce the reversal intended by God. Meier believes that these are the core beatitudes that derive from Jesus:

> Happy are the poor for theirs is the kingdom of
>   heaven.
> Happy are the mourners for they shall be
>   comforted.
> Happy are the hungry for they shall be satisfied.

The coming of God's rule will reverse the fortunes of the poor, the mourners, and the hungry. But Jesus is not here announcing a program for social reform. When Jesus speaks of the coming of God's rule, he means the end of the present age, when God's values will prevail because God wills it. "What human kings have not done and apparently will never do in Israel, God the king will do on the last day. . . . The core beatitudes indeed declare a revolution, but it is a revolution wrought by God alone as this present world comes to an end" (Meier, v. II, 331). Jesus is not a social reformer, but a prophet speaking about God and what God intends. It may be of interest to speak with Jesus about his seeming reticence in speaking out on the social issues of his day, namely, slavery, the Roman occupation of Palestine, the economic policies and social structures that led to the destitution of so many. His preoccupation was with God and what God would do, it seems, not with what he and his disciples might do to change situations of social evil.

This picture of the historical Jesus may give credence to Karl Marx's critique of Christianity as the "opiate of the people." Religion can seem to lead to the conclusion that followers of Jesus need be concerned only about the rule of God to come, that they should not concern themselves too much with social and political realities of the present age. When I put this issue to Jesus in prayer, I was immediately reminded that the historical Jesus used all the talents and powers he possessed to help the people he met. In a subsequent chapter we shall look in more detail at the miracles of the historical Jesus; for now we need to realize that another well-attested fact about him is that he was considered, and considered himself, a wonder worker. Did he not say to the disciples of John: "Go and tell John what you hear and see: the blind receive their sight, the lame walk, the lepers are cleansed, the deaf hear, the dead are raised, and the poor have good news brought to them" (Matt 11:2-5)? If Jesus were only interested in the transcendent rule of God to come, he would hardly have had any reason to care about the ills of this world.

Obviously Jesus believed that God did not want people to be blind, lame, leprous, deaf, or demon-possessed; he did what he could to eradicate these maladies when he encountered them. Moreover, these wonders were seen by Jesus as signs that the end time, the rule of God, had come near.

The Kingdom Is Already Present

The historical Jesus not only spoke of the coming of God's rule, that is, of its not-yet quality, but he also spoke as though God's rule were already made present by his own ministry. One indication is the response to John's disciples just cited. Here are a few others that are considered to have come in some fashion from the lips of the historical Jesus. In a dispute about the source of his power to cast out demons, Jesus said: "But if it is by the finger of God that I cast out the demons, then the kingdom of God has come to you" (Luke 11:20). Talk of exorcisms makes us nervous, but there is no question that Jesus believed he was casting out demons, and that his contemporaries, at least some of them, also thought so. Moreover, Jesus here says that his action of casting out demons indicates that the final rule of God has already begun.

On another occasion Jesus was asked when the kingdom was coming. He replied: "The kingdom of God is not coming with things that can be observed; nor will they say, 'Look, here it is!' or 'There it is!' For, in fact, the kingdom of God is among you" (Luke 17:20-21). As part of the sayings of Jesus about John the Baptist contained in Matthew and Luke there is an enigmatic statement about the kingdom of God and violence (Matt 11:12-13; Luke 16:16). On the basis of a careful exegesis Meier suggests that the original saying that was the source for both Matthew and Luke looked something like this: "The law and the prophets (lasted?) until John. From then on, the kingdom of God suffers violence, and the violent plunder it" (v. II, 403). These texts indicate that Jesus was convinced that with his ministry, a ministry both of proclamation and of actions such as exorcisms and healings, the rule of God had already broken into this world.

Moreover, this rule of God is suffering violent opposition, and that opposition is, of course, aimed at Jesus. Meier notes:

> The kingdom of God could not be suffering violent opposition as Jesus speaks if it had not taken on concrete, visible form in the words and deeds of Jesus. The very idea of the kingdom of God suffering from such violence is an astounding notion, foreign to the OT, the intertestamental literature, and the rest of the NT. The idea implies that what is in essence transcendent, eternal, invisible, and almighty—God's kingly rule—has somehow become immanent, temporal, visible, and vulnerable in Jesus' ministry (v. II, 403).

If Jesus were merely preaching a transcendent rule of God, a rule that had little or nothing to do with the social, political and religious realities of his time, then he would hardly have stirred up such violent animosity. Moreover, there would have been little incentive to attack him or his ministry. Jesus' preaching and ministry hardly fit Marx's description as the opiate of the people. Obviously the religious and political powers thought that he was anything but a soporific.

Further Reflections on Jesus

What does all this tell us about the historical Jesus? We are beginning to get a sense of a very complex consciousness. Jesus does not fit neatly into any preconceived categories. I wonder whether I would be embarrassed, for example, to be seen in the entourage of someone who openly asserted that he was casting out demons. Would I, like his family, wonder about his mental state? "When his family heard it, they went out to restrain him, for people were saying, 'He has gone out of his mind'" (Mark 3:21). How do we react to someone who baldly asserts that his message and his actions are, in effect, bringing on God's final, transcendent rule? What does it mean for Jesus to hold together in tension the belief that God's rule is transcendent, other-worldly, and due to God alone and the belief that he himself and his actions are central to God's rule? Moreover, how does he deal with the opposition, growing ever more violent, that his life and ministry evoked—opposition, mind you, from the religious leaders of his people? There is certainly material for dialogue with Jesus here.

It may not be amiss at this point to reflect on Jesus' relation to the social and religious structures of his era. I want to put this reflection in the context of our own age and its complexities. Since the Second Vatican Council many Christians have become accustomed to thinking that action to change unjust social structures is constitutive of being a follower of Jesus. My own tendency has been to equate the efforts to change such unjust social structures with what God wants, in other words, as part of God's rule. Thus, I have considered efforts, my own and those of others, to make political, social, and religious structures more just as at least part of God's work to bring about the kingdom. I have tended to see successes in these efforts as grace in operation to bring about God's rule. There is a certain similarity in this sort of thinking to the way Jesus seemed to conceive of his own ministry. I have not been foolish enough to equate the achievements for a more just society with God's kingdom; God's rule is still far from being fulfilled in this world. But I have noticed in myself—and have wondered whether it is true of others—that I get discouraged when efforts to bring about a more just society seem to be derailed.

In addition, I tend to equate certain political policies and the parties that espouse them with the work of God. Moreover, even when I believe that I have done all that I can to decide on a course of action in tune with God's desire, I tend to worry about the details, to be concerned about how everyone else will cooperate with what I have decided to do, even to contemplate how I might manipulate events so that the outcome I want (and believe is God's will) will occur. As a result, I am often not at peace even after coming to a peaceful decision about how to act in this world. Here contemplation of the historical Jesus may help.

We have already seen that Jesus did what he could to alleviate the misery that to his mind was foreign to what God's rule intends. He healed the sick, cast out demons, raised the dead, and equated these actions with the coming of God's rule. Moreover, he cared passionately about how people lived out the Law of God. For example, it is generally accepted that the historical Jesus did carry out a prophetic cleansing of the Temple (Mark 11:15-17); it mattered to him how people acted in the house of God. In addition, he condemned the religious posturing of some of the leaders of his own religion:

> "But woe to you Pharisees! For you tithe mint and rue and herbs of all kinds, and neglect justice and the love of God; it is these you ought to have practiced, without neglecting the others. Woe to you Pharisees! For you love to have the seat of honor in the synagogues and to be greeted with respect in the marketplaces. Woe to you! For you are like unmarked graves, and people walk over them without realizing it" (Luke 11:42-44).

And, if Meier is correct, Jesus took a mocking tone toward the lifestyle of King Herod when he was speaking of John the Baptist: "Look, those who put on fine clothing and live in luxury are in royal palaces" (Luke 7:25), thus indicating that he cared how rulers lived and what they did or did not do for their people. There are abundant indications that Jesus had a passionate interest in how people lived in this world because, it seems, Jesus felt he knew what God's rule intends. For example, there is sound evidence that Jesus took a very hard line regarding divorce; "Anyone who divorces his wife and marries another commits adultery, and whoever marries a woman divorced from her husband commits adultery" (Luke 16:18; see also, 1 Cor 7:10-11; Mark 10:2-12). This prohibition seemed so difficult that early Christians added riders (see Matt 5:32, 19:9; 1 Cor 7:15).

But how did Jesus react to the failure of his efforts and to the continuing injustice, poverty, suffering, and sinfulness of so many of God's people? Here, I believe, we find a reaction different from the discouragement and worry over the details I have noted in myself and which may, perhaps, occur in many others. Jesus seems to have had a profound trust in God's provident care, a belief that God would come to rule. He did not put the focus on himself but on God's initiative. Moreover, he seems to have accepted the shipwreck of his ministry with an equanimity that dazzles the beholder. In a Lenten article Monica Furlong speaks of working on the virtue of patience. She describes what it might be like to have this virtue.

> It is paradoxically about being no more than an in-significant drop whose passing will be only an eddy on the surface—less than a frog swallowed by a heron—yet knowing that within one the whole pattern of love is present and redemption already achieved. Within this love it is possible to rest in utter relaxation as a contented baby sleeps on its mother's lap (*The Tablet*, March 4, 1995, 284).

The kind of patience Monica Furlong hopes for, Jesus seems to have had. Jesus could live "as if everything needful has already been done" (Furlong quoting a rabbi on what it means to rest on the sabbath). In other words God has already done and is doing everything needful. I am reminded of a saying attributed to Ignatius of Loyola: "Pray as if everything depended on you; work as if everything depended on God." The idea is that we pray to discern how to act in this world in accordance with God's intention because it is very important that we act well, but once we have decided on a course of action we can leave everything in the hands of God, as Jesus seems to have done. God will write straight with whatever crooked lines we provide, whether we succeed in our efforts or not. Moreover, only God can move others to cooperate with our best actions for the common good. Jesus seems to have had the grace to believe this to an extraordinary degree. There is much here for our dialogue with Jesus.

Are We Blessed?

Before ending this chapter on Jesus' use of the kingdom of God symbol, let us look at one more saying that Meier considers to have some authenticity as a saying of Jesus. "Then turning to the disciples, Jesus said to them privately, 'Blessed are the eyes that see what you see! For I tell you that many prophets and kings desired to see what you see, but did not see it, and to hear what you hear, and did not hear it'" (Luke 10:23-24). Jesus congratulates his disciples for experiencing something the great ones of Israel had hoped for but had not experienced. Recall that the beatitudes make the same claim about the poor. Jesus' disciples live now in the fulfillment of the hopes of the prophets; they are experiencing the rule of God in fact.

Could it be that Jesus is so caught up in the action of God that he experiences now the fulfillment of that rule and thus is truly blessed? Could it be that Jesus believes that anyone who experiences his presence in faith also experiences that fulfillment and so is truly blessed? On the face of it, that seems the plain sense of this passage, taken in conjunction with the passages we have earlier examined. Now a further question: Could it be that the followers of Jesus down through the ages can have the same experience? Not that the historical Jesus was thinking of this possibility necessarily; rather, the question is an empirical one. Do we experience the beatitude of God's rule now? Have people had such experiences? Here I invite readers to reflect on their own experience or on the experience of others whom they have known.

Let me give some examples. In the diary left behind when she was hauled off to die in Auschwitz the Dutch Jewess Etty Hillesum leaves a testimony to her inner life as she faced her own and her people's utter destruction by the Nazis who had invaded Holland. Here is one of her entries, one that seems of a piece with the joy Jesus promised.

> But above the one narrow path still left to us stretches the sky, intact. They can't do anything to us, they really can't. They can harass us, they can rob us of our material goods, of our freedom of movement, but we ourselves forfeit our greatest assets by our misguided compliance. By our feelings of being persecuted, humiliated, and oppressed. By our own hatred. . . . We may of course be sad and depressed by what has been done to us; that is only human and understandable. However: our greatest injury is one we inflict upon ourselves. I find life beautiful and I feel free. The sky within me is as wide as the one stretching above my head. I believe in God and I believe in man and I say so without embarrassment. Life is hard, but that is no bad thing. . . . True peace will come only when every individual finds peace within himself; when we have all vanquished and transformed our hatred for our fellow human beings of whatever race—even into love one day, although perhaps that is asking too much. It is, however, the only solution. I am a happy person and I hold life dear indeed, in this year of Our Lord 1942, the umpteenth year of the war (*An Interrupted Life*, 151).

Another example comes from a poor black share-cropper from the American South who was put in jail for union activity in the 1930s. Now an old man, he is telling his story to Theodore Rosengarten and describes what happened to him in jail.

And all of a sudden, God stepped in my soul. Talk about hollerin and rejoicin, I just caught fire. My mind cleared up. I got so happy—I didn't realize where I was at. . . . And the Master commenced a talkin to me just like a natural man. I heard these words plain . . . "Follow me and trust me for my holy righteous word." I just gone wild then, feelin a change. . . . I commenced a shoutin bout the Lord, how good and kind and merciful He was. Freed my soul from sin. . . . Well, they had my trial and put me in prison. The Lord blessed my soul and set me in a position to endure it (Rosengarten, *All God's Dangers: The Life of Nate Shaw*, 333-34).

A final example comes from the German Lutheran pastor and theologian Dietrich Bonhoeffer, who was imprisoned and sentenced to death after the unsuccessful attempt on Hitler's life. In one of his last letters to a friend he wrote:

Please don't ever get anxious or worried about me, but don't forget to pray for me. . . . I am so sure of God's guiding hand that I hope I shall be kept in that certainty. You must never doubt that I'm traveling with gratitude and cheerfulness along the road where I'm being led. My past life is brimful of God's goodness, and my sins are covered by the forgiving love of Christ crucified. Forgive my writing this. Don't let it grieve or upset you for a moment, but let it make you happy. But I did want to say it for once, and I could not think of anyone else who I could be sure would take it aright (quoted in *The Tablet*, April 8, 1995, from *A Third Testament* by Malcolm Muggeridge).

Is it not true that many people experience an incredible joy even in the midst of great pain, and attribute the joy to the belief that all is well? Is it not possible that in these moments of bliss we experience what Jesus experienced and what Jesus attributed to his audience? Perhaps we too might want to pray to live, at least for moments, "as if everything needful had already been done," to live, at least for moments, in the cloud with the conviction of Julian of Norwich: "It behooveth that there should be sin: but all shall be well, and all shall be well, and all manner of thing shall be well" (*Revelations of Divine Love*, ch. 27, the 13th revelation).

Jesus the 4 Miracle Worker

"Go and tell John what you hear and see: the blind receive their sight, the lame walk, the lepers are cleansed, the deaf hear, the dead are raised, and the poor have good news brought to them" (Matt 11:4). In the last chapter we referred to this text and also indicated that one of the surest things that can be said by an unbiased historian about the historical Jesus is that he was considered and considered himself to be a miracle worker. In this chapter we want to look at some of the examples of gospel miracle stories that are considered to have some foundation in the life of the historical Jesus. Even though we are looking at the gospel texts with the eyes of a historian, we look at Jesus with the eyes of faith, hope, and love. Our desire is to know and love him better.

Again, we begin this search with the expression of our desire: "I want to know more about you so that I may love you more intensely and walk with you more closely."

Meier makes a very valid point; namely, no historian as such can say that an event was miraculous. Only a person of faith can attest that an out-of-the-ordinary event is a miracle, because, as he says, "it is of the essence of a miracle that the event is seen to have as its only adequate cause and explanation a special act of God, who alone is able to bring about the miraculous effect" (v. II, 513). Meier notes that historians or scientists may say that the event has no known explanation, as does, for example, the International Medical Committee located in Paris about some cures that occur at Lourdes. But only those scientists or historians who have faith can then go on to say, "This is an act of God."

Now it must be said that many modern academics operate with the unspoken creed that was once formulated by the German scriptural scholar Rudolph Bultmann: "It is impossible to use electric light and 'the wireless,' and to avail ourselves of modern medical and surgical discoveries, and at the same time to believe in the New Testament world of . . . miracles" (cited in Meier, v. II, 520). Bultmann's statement purports to be an empirical fact, but is it true? Meier refers to a Gallup poll of 1989 which found that eighty-two percent of Americans polled (all of whom, it is presumed, use electric light and the wireless and some of whom may even be scientists and professors) believe that "even today, miracles are performed by the power of God" (*ibid.*). We need not cede to the unbeliever or the agnostic the higher ground in the argument about either the existence of God or the possibility of miracles. An unbeliever denies the possibility of either on philosophical grounds, not on empirical proof. On these questions believers and unbelievers both plant their feet firmly in the air and march on; that is, both make "leaps of faith" that are not grounded on empirical evidence. As we approach the wonders attributed to the historical Jesus, it is well to remember that the presumption against the miraculous has no more solid footing than the presumption for the miraculous.

Jesus the Exorcist

In the last chapter we noted that one of Jesus' sayings that has a ring of historical authenticity concerns the casting out of demons: "But if it is by the finger of God that I cast out the demons, then the kingdom of God has come to you" (Luke 11:20). There are at least a few stories of exorcisms that Meier believes refer back to some event in Jesus' life. For example, the following story may represent the fact that Jesus did perform some exorcisms at Capernaum, a town that came to be his home base, as it were.

> Just then there was in their synagogue a man with an unclean spirit, and he cried out, "What have you to do with us, Jesus of Nazareth? Have you come to destroy us? I know who you are, the Holy One of God." But Jesus rebuked him, saying, "Be silent, and come out of him!" And the unclean spirit, convulsing him and crying with a loud voice, came out of him. They were all amazed, and they kept on asking one another, "What is this? A new teaching—with authority! He commands even the unclean spirits, and they obey him." At once his fame began to spread throughout the surrounding region of Galilee (Mark 1:23-28).

In Luke we read that among those with Jesus was "Mary, called Magdalene, from whom seven demons had gone out" (Luke 8:2). Given that in all four gospels Mary Magdalene becomes one of the chief witnesses of the resurrection, Meier believes it highly unlikely that the early church invented the story that she had been demon-possessed. To do so would have raised questions about her credibility. He surmises that the story of her exorcism must have been current during Jesus' life and could not have been denied. He also inclines to the opinion that there is some historical basis to the story in Mark 9:14-29 of the possessed boy whom Jesus exorcises and to the story in Mark 5:1-20 of the exorcism of the Gerasene demoniac.

If you read these scenes contemplatively and ask to experience the power of the confrontations, you will get a sense of the epic struggle between Jesus and a personified power of evil. These scenes contain images of raw rage, of superhuman strength, of uncanny insight. Yet Jesus faces the possessed person with a calm and commanding presence. As we contemplate these scenes, we can ask Jesus to help us to feel what he feels or, at least, to have some inkling of what he experiences. Perhaps we can sense the dismay of the onlookers, "What is this? A new teaching—with authority! He commands even the unclean spirits, and they obey him" (Mark 1:27).

What are we to make of these very strange happenings? Meier and many modern exegetes believe that the symptoms ascribed to the possessed boy in Mark 9 can be explained as epilepsy. Even if this is granted, the issue remains: What did Jesus make of this poor boy's affliction and of the other afflicted people whom he exorcised? It would appear that he believed that he was indeed casting out demons. Thus Jesus lived in a world where evil was a personified power greater than any human agency. When we contemplate the scenes where Jesus confronts demonic power, therefore, we need to ask him to help us to empathize with him. In spite of our hesitations before the demonic, perhaps we who have lived through the horrors of this century—who have read and seen pictures and films of the ghastly trench warfare of World War I; of the Holocaust, fire bombings, and atom bombings of World War II; of Vietnam and the killing fields of Cambodia; of the grisly murders of innocent people by military governments in Latin America; of the "ethnic cleansing" in the former Yugoslavia; of the effects of terrorist bombings in Northern Ireland, Great Britain, the United States, and elsewhere; of the physical and sexual abuse and murder of women and children throughout the world— perhaps we can have some sense of an evil power that seems inhuman, indeed diabolical.

What was it like for Jesus to face the violence, rage, and unpredictability of those who were deemed to be possessed by demons? As we contemplate Jesus, we might want to ask him to help us to be unafraid before the power of evil, to be more willing to stand up to it because of an increased faith in the greater power of God. In a passage where he is responding to the charge that he cast out demons by the power of the ruler of the demons, Jesus is purported to say: "But no one can enter a strong man's house and plunder his property without first tying up the strong man; then indeed the house can be plundered" (Mark 3:27). In effect, Jesus is saying that he represents the stronger power, namely God; hence he can plunder the house of Satan. Thus he can say: "But if it is by the finger of God that I cast out the demons, then the kingdom of God has come to you" (Luke 11:20). Let me quote William Barclay's commentary on Mark 3:27:

Jesus accepts life as a struggle between the power of evil and the power of God. He did not waste his time in speculations about problems to which there is no answer. He did not stop to argue about where evil came from; but he did deal with it most effectively. One of the odd things is that we spend a good deal of time discussing the origin of evil; but we spend less time working out practical methods of tackling the problem. . . . Jesus saw the essential struggle between good and evil which is at the heart of life and raging in the world. He did not speculate about it; he dealt with it and gave to others the power to overcome evil and do the right (*The Gospel of Mark: Revised Edition,* 78-79).

We might want to ask Jesus for help to have his attitude in the face of evil and thus be freed of wasting time and energy speculating about the origins of evil.

We can also see how the early church used stories of exorcisms to make points about its mission. Earlier I noted that I had considered the story of the Syrophoenician woman (Mark 7:24-30; Matt 15:21-28) as going back to the historical Jesus. Meier looks at the evidence and concludes (not without some hesitation) that the story was developed by the early church to buttress its missionary theology, that is, the expansion of its mission to the Gentiles whom this woman of great faith represents. With the exorcism stories we see how Christians take a real attribute of the historical Jesus— that he was considered an exorcist—to help them to make sense of the totally new situation presented by the expansion of Christianity beyond Israel.

What about our own times? As I was writing this section, I began to ask Jesus about situations I have faced, situations of seemingly intractable psychological illness, for example. I began to recall times when I faced the seeming black hole of depression in another person. A composite picture may help. The man was forty years old. He felt that he was a failure, that he was unloved and unlovable. He saw nothing but blackness ahead in life and had thought of suicide. He had been in psychotherapy a number of times, but it had not been of much help. For him, God was an implacable hounder of sinners, and he was one of the hounded ones. He had tried everything to put things right with God—novenas, rosaries, pilgrimages, confessions. He was also quite scrupulous, worrying, for example, about particles of hosts, involuntary thoughts and images, and the like.

When I was his spiritual director, I had no answers, only the blind trust that God was a loving God and that somehow he had had experiences of this loving God. Hence I tried to get him to recall incidents when he had been happy, when he had not been feeling so dismal. I asked him to focus on such times as telling him something different about God. In recalling instances that go to make up this composite profile, I feel that I was given the grace to stand before the power of darkness in a way somewhat analogous to Jesus' way. I also recall one incident where I wondered whether Jesus might have expected me to go further, to take the step of praying aloud for healing and of laying on my hands, a step I did not take. Was my reluctance an excess of prudence or prudence itself? Hard to be sure, but I tend to think, in retrospect, that it was the former.

I was also reminded of a scene in George Bernanos's novel *Diary of a Country Priest*. One of the main characters, the Countess, lost her only son, the light of her life, when he was a child. Her husband is a philanderer; her daughter has fastened all her affections on her father and excluded her mother from their circle. The Countess harbors a deep resentment and hatred for her husband and her daughter, but because of her position she has never let anyone, even her confessor, know. Outwardly she has kept the proprieties. In the climactic scene with the country priest they talk about the fact that her daughter is being sent away to England by her husband because the daughter is jealous about the affair her father is having with her governess. In this dialogue it comes out that the Countess believes that the daughter will commit suicide if forced to go. In her hatred she will do nothing to prevent this outcome.

The country priest then touches the neuralgic point of her hatred, her bitter resentment at the death of her son. He tells her that her hatred will keep her separated from her son forever. This leads to another outpouring of venom ending with the priest pointing to the peril she is in. He goes on to tell her that secret sins poison the air, thus indicating that at least some of the hatred in her daughter may be due to her own hidden sin. She says:

"Would you deign to show me my hidden sin? The worm in the fruit?"

"You must resign yourself to—to God. Open your heart to Him."

I dared not speak more plainly of her dead child, and the word "resign" seemed to astonish her.

"Resign myself? To what?" Then suddenly she understood. . . .

"Resign myself?" Her gentle voice froze. "What do

82

you mean? Don't you think me resigned enough? If I hadn't been resigned! It makes me ashamed. . . . I tell you I've often envied weaker women who haven't the strength to toil up these hills. But we're such a tough lot! I should have killed my wretched body, so that it shouldn't forget. Not all of us can manage to kill ourselves—"

"That's not the resignation I mean, as you well know," I said to her.

"Well then—what? I go to mass, I make my Easter (duty). I might have given up going to church altogether—I did think of it at one time. But I considered that sort of thing beneath me."

"Madame, no blasphemy you could utter would be as bad as what you've just said! Your words have all the callousness of hell in them. . . . How dare you treat God in such a way? You close your heart against him and you —"

"At least I've lived in peace—and I might have died in it—"

"That's no longer possible."

She reared like a viper: "I've ceased to bother about God. When you've forced me to admit that I hate him, will you be any better off, you idiot?"

"You no longer hate him. Hate is indifference and contempt. Now at last you're face to face with him."

The scene goes on. She faces the fact that she has never really given up her son, has tried to keep him by the force of her own will. She has not said the Our Father since the day he died because of the words, "Thy will be done." As she struggles to surrender to God, she feels that she is losing her son all over again. At the climax of the scene she says:

"I'll either give him all or nothing. My people are
made that way."

"Give everything."

"Oh, you don't understand! You think you've managed to make me docile. The dregs of my pride
would still be enough to send you to hell."

"Give your pride with all the rest! Give everything!"

In a desperate gesture, which the priest is unable to stop, she flings the medallion that contains a lock of her son's hair into the fire. But she is at peace. At the end of the novel, when the priest has died, we are told that his last words were, *"Tout est grace"* (All is grace). The novelist, I believe, is telling us how the priest could have lived the life he did and faced the almost diabolical rage of the Countess with such courage and hope. Perhaps we have here a literary example of someone given the grace to face the demonic with trust in the love of God.

Jesus the Healer

Jesus tells the disciples of John: "The blind receive their sight, the lame walk, the lepers are cleansed, the deaf hear, the dead are raised." In this section we want to look at some of these stories of Jesus the healer.

The Blind Receive Their Sight

In the gospels there are three stories about the healing of the blind: Bartimaeus (Mark 10:46-52), the blind man at Bethsaida (Mark 8:22-26), and the man born blind (John 9). Meier concludes that all three "reflect events in Jesus' ministry" (v. II, 969). Since I have used the story of Bartimaeus often in homilies, articles, and books, I was heartened to read that it is one of the strongest candidates for being the report of a specific miracle to a named person. It might be useful for our contemplation of the historical Jesus to look carefully at this story and especially at the elements that, according to Meier, seem to go back to the time of Jesus.

This blind man is named Bartimaeus. No other recipient of a healing miracle apart from the twelve apostles is named in any of the gospels. The fact of his being named argues to his having been a real historical character in the life of Jesus. In addition, the tradition available to Mark used his Aramaic name without any explanation. Since Mark is writing for a Gentile audience, he translates the name as "son of Timaeus" for them. The tradition also recalls the Aramaic title given by Bartimaeus to Jesus—"Rabbouni," that is, "my master" or "my teacher."

The locale of the miracle also argues for its historical origin. Pilgrims who came up to the Holy City from Galilee for the celebration of Passover most often avoided going through Samaria. Hence, they crossed to the other side of the Jordan in Galilee, walked south along the river, crossed again and entered the town of Jericho, and from there headed toward Jerusalem, some twenty miles to the east. Almsgiving was a part of the pilgrimage to Jerusalem. A smart beggar would position himself on the outskirts of Jericho, where the pilgrims left the town and started on the road that climbed toward Jerusalem. This is the locale of the story.

Finally, Bartimaeus calls Jesus "Son of David," a name Meier traces to its Old Testament and later Jewish roots in the stories of Solomon, the "son of David" who was well known as a healer, exorcist, and miracle worker. Meier thinks it not unlikely that afflicted people of the time began to see Jesus as a modern version of the miracle-working Solomon, the "son of David." These, then, are the elements that may well have comprised the "facts" of the original event and that led to the story we now have in the gospel of Mark.

Readers can use these elements to know Jesus better. Imagine the scene as the crowds of pilgrims leave Jericho and begin the climb toward Jerusalem. Bartimaeus is only one of the beggars waiting for the pilgrims. How does Jesus react to all these beggars? How does the crowd react? What happens in Jesus as he hears himself publicly called "Son of David" and "Rabbouni?" How does he react to the naked desire of this man to receive back his sight? And how would he want a follower of his in our age to react to beggars and to the afflicted? What goes on in Jesus as he contemplates this blind man and the possibility that he might cure him? What does it mean to sense in himself the power to heal? How do I react to his words, "Go; your faith has made you well"? Perhaps I am feeling the awe that often overwhelmed the crowds when Jesus worked wonders, "We have never seen anything like this!"(Mark 2:12). Contemplation of Jesus' experiences in this way certainly suggests much that could be brought to conversation with him.

As noted earlier, Meier also believes that the cure of the blind man at Bethsaida (Mark 8:22-26) has a historical substratum. Two elements stand out in his argument and make striking matter for contemplation. According to Meier the most accurate translation of what Jesus does to cure the blind man is this: "And spitting into his eyes, placing [his] hands on him, he asked him, 'Can you see anything?'" We know that the man is not completely cured the first time, and so Jesus has to repeat the treatment before a full cure is achieved. As Meier says, "To put it as delicately as possible: having Jesus spit in a person's face does not seem to fit any stream of christology in the early church. Moreover, nowhere else in the NT does Jesus' healing action fail to have its full effect immediately and therefore need to be repeated" (v. II, 693). When I told this story to a very religious woman, her immediate reaction was, "How gross!" The historical Jesus is obviously not of the social and cultural class of most of the readers of this book or of the author. Some of us might recognize the need of God's grace to get close to this marginal Jew of the first century of our era.

With these two stories we are also in the position of noting how Mark uses these cures creatively for his own theological purposes. He puts the cure of the blind man at Bethsaida right after Jesus has berated the disciples for their blindness in not understanding the miracle of the multiplication of the loaves. Moreover, it begins a very important section of the gospel that concludes with the cure of Bartimaeus, thus forming what in classical rhetoric was called an *inclusio,* a section of a narrative or speech bounded by two similar stories or figures of speech.

Right after the first cure of a blind man Peter has his spiritual sight partly healed so that he can respond with faith to Jesus' question "But who do you say that I am?" Peter answers, "You are the Messiah" (Mark 8:29). But his sight is only partial because he misses the point when Jesus explains that his messiahship means crucifixion and death. He begins to remonstrate with Jesus, and Jesus in anger and in the strongest terms rebukes him, "Get behind me, Satan!" (Mark 8:33). Indeed, in this central section of Mark's gospel Jesus three times predicts his passion only to find that the disciples are blind to his meaning; Peter remonstrates with him after the first prediction (Mark 8:32), the disciples argue over who was the greatest after the second (Mark 9:34), and James and John ask to sit at his right and left in the kingdom and the other disciples get angry with them after the third (Mark 10:35-37, 41). The section concludes with the cure of Bartimaeus, who not only is cured immediately of his blindness, but becomes for the writer of the gospel the prototype of the Christian. "He followed (Jesus) on the way" (Mark 10:52), where "the way" refers to Jesus' way of the cross which is about to begin, and to the Christian life. Early Christians were called "people of the Way."

Thus the final writer of Mark's gospel takes two stories that refer back to the historical Jesus and uses and embellishes them not only to witness to Jesus but also to make his theological point that Jesus can only be seen truly in and through the crucifixion. In Mark the first human affirmation of who Jesus really is comes from the Gentile centurion who sees him breathe his last on the cross: "Truly this man was God's Son!" (Mark 15:39).

We might want to ask Jesus to give us our sight again so that we might know and love him and follow him more closely, but also so that we might be able to see our world through his eyes. Physical blindness is still with us, a sign that the fullness of God's rule is still in the future. But more important, spiritual blindness is even more prevalent, a blindness that keeps us from seeing that this universe is God's creation and is governed by God's intention, a blindness that keeps us from doing what we can to let God achieve his intention. We will not, however, be able to act with hope and confidence in tune with God's intention if we do not see that in spite of everything this universe is "charged with the grandeur of God," as the poet Gerard Manley Hopkins put it in his wonderful poem:

> The world is charged with the grandeur of God.
>> It will flame out, like shining from shook foil;
>> It gathers to a greatness, like the ooze of oil
> Crushed. Why do men then now not reck his rod?
> Generations have trod, have trod, have trod;
>> And all is seared with trade; bleared, smeared
>> with toil;
>> And wears man's smudge and shares man's
>> smell: the soil
> Is bare now, nor can foot feel, being shod.
>
> And for all this, nature is never spent;
>> There lives the dearest freshness deep down
>> things;
> And though the last lights off the black West went
>> Oh, morning, at the brown brink eastwards,
>> springs—
> Because the Holy Ghost over the bent
>> World broods with warm breast and with ah!
>> bright wings.

The world is indeed "bent"; it is bent by sin and evil out of the shape God intends, and it is bent as an egg over which a hen broods is bent (into an oval.) Yet in spite of its "bentness," indeed, perhaps because of its "bentness," God will still bring to birth the wonder God intends. If we have that hope, that vision of our world, then we will have the energy to cooperate with God's grace to achieve what God wants. Obviously the historical Jesus saw the world as it really was, accepted its full reality, yet still believed that God would write straight with its crooked lines.

The Lame Walk

Meier concludes that two of the four stories of the healing of physical paralysis have roots in events in Jesus' life. (An aside: When Meier concludes that some stories have a historical basis, he does not necessarily mean that the others have none; all that we can say of these others is that we cannot decide whether they had such a basis. It is not necessary to conclude that the early church made up these stories out of whole cloth.) Let's take a look at the two he mentions.

At the beginning of the second chapter of Mark (2:1-12) we read of the paralyzed man whose friends carry him up onto the flat roof of the house where Jesus is, dig through the mud and thatch roof, and let him down with ropes into the house. Meier thinks that

> some event in the public ministry stuck in the corporate memory precisely because of its strange circumstances. Moreover, if one should allow that Jesus' assurance that the man's sins were forgiven formed part of the original story, this element would make the narrative practically unique among the miracle stories of the gospels (v. II, 680).

The element of controversy with the scribes may be an addition of the writer of the gospel since the story is placed among a series of stories of controversy that lead to the ominous statement at the end of this section of the gospel: "The Pharisees went out and immediately conspired with the Herodians against him, how to destroy him" (Mark 3:6). As we contemplate this scene, we note that it is said that Jesus saw the faith of the man's friends and that this faith led him first to say that the man's sins were forgiven and then to heal the man of his paralysis. How did Jesus react to these friends and to the paralytic? Our contemplation might tell us something about how moved Jesus was by their faith and by their willingness to put that faith into an action that took a good deal of exertion on their part. How did the crowd through which they had to push greet their efforts? Good Samaritans are not always rewarded for their kindness.

The other story is contained in the gospel of John:

After this there was a festival of the Jews, and Jesus went up to Jerusalem. Now in Jerusalem by the Sheep Gate there is a pool, called in Hebrew Beth-za-tha, which has five porticoes. In these lay many in-valids—blind, lame, and paralyzed. One man was there who had been ill for thirty-eight years. When Jesus saw him lying there and knew that he had been there a long time, he said to him, "Do you want to be made well?" The sick man answered him, "Sir, I have no one to put me into the pool when the water is stirred up; and while I am making my way, someone else steps down ahead of me." Jesus said to him, "Stand up, take your mat, and walk." At once the man was made well, and he took up his mat and be-gan to walk (John 5:1-9).

The details about the actual location of the pool in Jerusalem prior to its destruction in 70 A.D., some of which recently have been shown to be accurate through excavations, argue for an early development of the story and thus for an event in the life of Jesus. The gospel writer embellishes the story he received from the tradition and adds at the end that this healing occurred on the sabbath, a device to increase the element of menace from the authorities. In the gospel they become incensed because the miracle is said to have occurred on the sabbath. But we can take this story in John's gospel, along with the story of the man born blind in chapter 9, as having some foundation in the life of Jesus himself. As Meier says, it would be surprising if Jesus, who seems to have come up to Jerusalem a few times for holy days, did not do some healing there; these are the only two healing stories in the gospels that are said to have occurred in Jerusalem.

What was it like for Jesus to exercise his healing ministry in the Holy City itself, the city which still exercises such a pull on religious people of three different faiths, Jews, Muslims, and Christians? Here was the rebuilt Temple of Solomon, the center of worship of the God of Israel. Jesus himself must have prayed such psalms as Psalm 84, with its expression of desire to be in God's temple:

How lovely is your dwelling place,
　O Lord of hosts!
My soul longs, indeed it faints
　for the courts of the Lord;
my heart and my flesh sing for joy
　to the living God.

Even the sparrow finds a home,
   and the swallow a nest for herself,
   where she may lay her young,
at your altars, O Lord of hosts,
   my King and my God.
Happy are those who live in your house,
   ever singing your praise (1-4).

He would have remembered the poignant psalm attributed to the exiles in Babylon:

By the rivers of Babylon—
   there we sat down and there we wept
   when we remembered Zion.
On the willows there
   we hung up our harps.
For there our captors
   asked us for songs,
and our tormentors asked for mirth, saying,
   "Sing us one of the songs of Zion!"
How could we sing the Lord's song
   in a foreign land?
If I forget you, O Jerusalem,
   let my right hand wither!
Let my tongue cling to the roof of my mouth,
   if I do not remember you,
if I do not set Jerusalem
   above my highest joy (Ps 137:1-6).

Moreover, with his consciousness of the imminence, indeed of the presence in his ministry of God's promised rule, would he not have recalled the promises of the prophets about Jerusalem, promises such as this from Second Isaiah?

How beautiful upon the mountains
    are the feet of the messenger who announces
    peace,
who brings good news,
    who announces salvation,
    who says to Zion, "Your God reigns."
Listen! Your sentinels lift up their voices,
    together they sing for joy;
for in plain sight they see
    the return of the Lord to Zion.
Break forth together into singing,
    you ruins of Jerusalem;
for the Lord has comforted his people,
    he has redeemed Jerusalem.
The Lord has bared his holy arm
    before the eyes of all the nations;
and all the ends of the earth shall see
    the salvation of our God (Is 52:7-10).

Given what we have already seen of the historical Jesus, it is not surprising that the early church either remembered or put into his mouth the following words as he approached Jerusalem, perhaps for the last time: "Jerusalem, Jerusalem, the city that kills the prophets and stones those who are sent to it! How often have I desired to gather your children together as a hen gathers her brood under her wings, and you were not willing!" (Luke 13:34). We can ask Jesus to help us to know his heart and mind as he preached and worked marvels in the Holy City.

We might be helped in appreciating Jesus' reactions by recalling our own reactions when we entered a special, awe-inspiring place, especially if we engaged in some ministry or assisted someone there. Michael Hollings describes the effect of ministering at Lourdes:

> There was much waiting, especially when we were left to help out during the night with delayed arrivals or departures. Chatting with the sick, helping them to be comfortable, opened the way to heart-to-heart confidences which spread to doctors and nurses. And then in between, through the night, in the open spaces of the landing field, ringed by mountains, there were glorious sunsets over the Lourdes mountains, the rising moon, the distant rattle of a train, the call of night birds. In the midst of tiredness and the joy of being with the sick, I used to snatch periods of lonely separation for contemplation as the world opened with stars, so as to be alone with God for short periods. . . .
>
> One of the important features of Lourdes is the development of relationships among and with the sick, doctors, nurses, helpers and brancardiers. In a relationship of prayer with Jesus and Mary, and with each other, and in a climate of companionship and personal growth, Lourdes is a seedbed for much that is best in Christian community building. As every one of us is created by God for a relationship of love with him and each other, we find the way is a mixture, because with joy there is sorrow, with giving, receiving; and for a Christian there must be prayer also. Lourdes gathers all these together (The Tablet, June 17, 1995, 771).

The Lepers Are Cleansed

There are two stories of the cleansing of lepers in the gospels, the healing of the leper in Mark 1:40-45 and the healing of the ten lepers in Luke 17:11-19. Meier points out that it is unlikely that the leprosy referred to in the gospels is what we know as Hansen's disease; the gospels could be referring to a number of skin diseases covered by the legislation of the Hebrew scriptures. Nonetheless, just as Elisha, one of the great prophets of the Old Testament, is depicted as curing leprosy, so too is Jesus. In spite of the arguments of some exegetes, Meier tends to believe that the attribution of the cure of leprosy to Jesus, and thus the consideration of him as, at the least, one of the prophets, go back to the time of the historical Jesus himself.

Meier, however, sees difficulties in tracing some of the details of the stories back to the historical Jesus. Thus, in the Markan story Jesus is depicted as reacting with very strong emotion and as touching the leper. The Lukan story of the ten lepers of whom only one, and he a Samaritan, returns to give thanks seems to have had considerable embellishments for Luke's theological purposes. For example, Luke, writing at a time when most Jews have rejected salvation through Jesus, underlines the fact that the despised Samaritan is the one who returns to give thanks and is rewarded by having Jesus give him not only physical healing but also spiritual healing: "Your faith has made you well" (Luke 17:19). The Greek word translated as "has made you well" has, according to Meier, the full sense of being saved. Again we see that a story about the historical Jesus is used by the early church and by a particular writer to make a theological or homiletic point for a particular audience.

For us who want to know Jesus better, the questions for contemplation might be these: How does Jesus experience this sense of being different from John the Baptist and the other prophetic figures of his time, this sense that he can, for example, cleanse lepers? What goes on in him as he becomes (progressively?) aware of himself as in the line of the great prophets like Elijah and Elisha? If ever you have experienced some kind of new power or gift in yourself, you may have an inkling of what Jesus might have experienced, and this inkling might be the vehicle Jesus uses to let you have some deeper knowledge of his own reactions.

An example: Once I was told that in my work as spiritual director with a particular person I had come across as someone who was anchored in the love of God, someone who clung to that love even when times were very bleak in the life of the directee, someone who could not be budged from that conviction but did not belabor the point uselessly. I need not go into all the details, nor do I recall the incident to glorify myself. I want to mention my reactions. I was awed by what this person told me, awed that I could be so perceived and had been helpful as a result; I was immensely grateful to God and to all those who had helped me to have such a faith-filled conviction; I felt satisfaction and even a bit of pride that I could have been used to convey to another person something about God's tremendous love. As a result of that experience I think I have been given some inkling of Jesus' human experience—of course only a very distant inkling.

In our day the scourge of HIV/AIDS has been likened to that of leprosy in the scriptures. There are similarities, not the least of which is the fact that those with HIV/AIDS suffer discrimination and ostracization. How would Jesus of Nazareth react to this modern scourge? Perhaps we get some idea from the experience of those who have lived with the syndrome or who have ministered to people who are HIV-positive. In an article in *The Tablet* (May 13, 1995) Kevin Kelly writes about some of the men and women he has met who are suffering with AIDS. One is an Asian woman he names Maria, the eldest girl in a family of thirteen. Maria was raped by her father while quite young. Feeling soiled and also feeling the need to earn money to help feed her brothers and sisters and parents, she took to prostitution and predictably found herself infected with HIV. She gave up prostitution and has devoted her life to working with a Catholic organization caring for those with AIDS and trying to educate others about the virus.

Kelly says: "Maria spoke openly to me about the suffering and eventual death that awaited her. . . . She said she trusted God absolutely and knew that he would be with her through whatever horrors she had to endure." He then went on to say:

> Some people might condemn Maria and say that it was her own fault that she has AIDS. God is punishing her for engaging in prostitution. Those words are more reminiscent of the sentiments of the scribes and Pharisees than of Jesus. I am sure Jesus' reading of Maria's situation would be far more profound. He would take account of the horrendous train of events and of the pressures which eventually drove her into dehumanizing prostitution. He would be able to penetrate the depths of her soul and would be deeply moved by her spirit of generous self-sacrifice. "Greater love has no one . . ." Before I left, Maria asked me to pray for her. I replied by asking her to

pray for me. I felt privileged when she promised she would. I believe that her prayers will carry greater weight before the Lord than mine.

Kelly then writes of three Thai men who contracted the virus through prostitution. When it became known that they were HIV-positive, they were ostracized and became destitute. Near death, they ended up in a Catholic AIDS hospice.

> Given loving and compassionate care and good nourishment in the hospice, all three of them have recovered for the time being and each of them is dedicating his life to working in Church-related projects concerned with HIV/AIDS prevention and education, as well as caring for HIV-positive men and women who, like themselves, have been abandoned by those closest to them. Once again, the dedication of all of them is heroic and the depth of their faith commitment is remarkable. On their own admission, the quality of their lives has been deepened enormously. Wimsol actually said to me, "AIDS is my gift," and Thaksin told the assembled theologians at our meeting, "To compare my life before HIV/AIDS and my life today, is like comparing night and day."

Jesus is still touching people in our day as he did when he cured lepers in first-century Palestine.

The Deaf Hear

There is only one story of a healing of a deaf person, the deaf-mute of Mark 7:31-37. With hesitation, but because of Jesus' use of Aramaic and again spittle, Meier is inclined to regard the story as having some relation to Jesus himself. I mention the story here for the sake of completeness and also because once again Jesus is shown using spit to effect a cure. He was not a sophisticated twentieth-century North American!

The Dead Are Raised

There is probably no miracle attributed to Jesus that evokes more skepticism than that of raising the dead. Jesus is depicted as having brought some people who had died back to life. The life to which they returned was not the resurrected life Jesus himself enjoys after Easter, but ordinary life in the body such as they enjoyed before they died. The question Meier tries to answer is not whether there was a real miracle, but whether the stories about the raising of the dead go back to the historical Jesus himself; that is, whether his contemporaries and Jesus himself thought that he did indeed raise some people from the dead.

Surprisingly, stories of such happenings are at least as widely attested to by the various sources as anything else attributed to the historical Jesus. "Historical judgments about individual stories are extremely difficult, but the multiple attestation of both sources and forms . . . argues that even during his lifetime Jesus was thought by his disciples to have raised the dead" (v. II, 970). Meier suggests that the story of the raising of the daughter of Jairus (Mark 5:21-43) goes back to some event in the life of Jesus and inclines to believe that the stories of the raising of the son of the widow of Nain (Luke 7:11-17) and of Lazarus (John 11:1-46) do also. Without, therefore, pressing any of these stories on their details we can say, on fairly good authority, that Jesus and his contemporaries thought that he had indeed raised the dead, much as Elijah and Elisha are said to have raised the dead. I might add that those who are said to have been raised from the dead died prematurely and left grieving parents and sisters; Jesus is depicted as acting out of compassion for the grieving.

The questions for contemplation of the historical Jesus might well be: How did he react to the mourning widow and to the parents of the little girl? What was his experience as he felt this tremendous power emanating from him? What kind of faith in God and in God's choice of him did he have to believe that through the power of God he could overcome our last enemy, death itself? What kind of man was this marginal Jew?

Jesus Still Heals

Reynolds Price, in his memoir, *A Whole New Life*, provides us with an example from our own day of Jesus bringing assurance of a cure. Price had had a very serious operation on his spinal cord and was recuperating so that he could then undergo massive radiation therapy for the significant cancerous tumor that remained. He recounts this incident:

> So by daylight on July 3rd, morning thoughts of a stiff sobriety were plainly in order. But in the midst of such circular thinking, an actual happening intervened with no trace of warning. I was suddenly not propped in my brass bed or even contained in my familiar house. By the dim new, thoroughly credible light that rose around me, it was barely dawn; and I was lying fully dressed in modern street clothes on a slope by a lake I knew at once. It was the big lake of Kinnereth, the Sea of Galilee, in the north of Israel—green Galilee, the scene of Jesus' first teaching and healing. I'd paid the lake a second visit the previous October, a twelve-mile-long body of fish-stocked wa-

ter in beautiful hills of grass, trees and small family farms.

Still sleeping around me on the misty ground were a number of men in the tunics and cloaks of first-century Palestine. I soon understood with no sense of surprise that the men were Jesus' twelve disciples and that he was nearby asleep among them. So I lay on a while in the early chill, looking west across the lake to Tiberias, a small low town, and north to the fishing villages of Capernaum and Bethsaida. I saw them as they were in the first century—stone huts with thatch-and-mud roofs, occasional low towers, the rising smoke of breakfast fires. The early light was a fine mix of tan and rose. It would be a fair day.

Then one of the sleeping men woke and stood.

I saw it was Jesus, bound toward me. He looked much like the lean Jesus of Flemish paintings—tall with dark hair, unblemished skin and a self-possession both natural and imposing.

Again I felt no shock or fear. All this was normal human event; it was utterly clear to my normal eyes and was happening as surely as any event of my previous life. I lay and watched him walk on nearer.

Jesus bent and silently beckoned me to follow.

I knew to shuck off my trousers and jacket, then my shirt and shorts. Bare, I followed him.

He was wearing a twisted white cloth round his loins; otherwise he was bare and the color of ivory.

We waded out into cool lake water twenty feet from shore till we stood waist-deep.

I was in my body but was also watching my body from slightly upward and behind. I could see the purple dye on my back, the long rectangle that boxed my thriving tumor.

Jesus silently took up handfuls of water and poured them over my head and back till water ran down my puckered scar. Then he spoke once—"Your sins are forgiven"—and turned to shore again, done with me.

I came on behind him, thinking in standard greedy fashion, It's not my sins I'm worried about. So to Jesus' receding back, I had the gall to say "Am I also cured?"

He turned to face me, no sign of a smile, and finally said two words—"That too." Then he climbed from the water, not looking round, really done with me.

I followed him out and then, with no palpable seam in the texture of time or place, I was home again in my wide bed (42-43).

Price recognizes the possibility that this was just a dream, even a wish-fulfillment dream. But he avers: "From the moment my mind was back in my own room, no more than seconds after I'd left, I've believed that the event was an external gift, however brief, of an alternate time and space in which to live through a crucial act" (44). He was eventually cured of the cancer, though only after much suffering, much radiation therapy, and another operation, and he was left paralyzed from the waist down. The last lines of his memoir describe his present life, which includes long days of writing. He ends the memoir with these words: "Even my handwriting looks very little like the script of the man I was in June of '84. Cranky as it is, it's taller, more legible, with more air and stride. It comes down the arm of a grateful man" (193).

Jesus in Control of Nature

In a few stories in the gospels Jesus is depicted as having some control over nature. He tells Peter to catch a fish in which he will find the coin for the Temple tax (Matt 17:24-27). He curses a fig tree, and it withers (Mark 11:12-14, 20-21). At his word fishermen make a miraculous catch of fish (Luke 5:1-11; John 21:1-14). He walks on water (Mark 6:45-52 , Matt 14:22-33). He stills a storm at sea (Mark 4:35-41, Matt 8:23-27, Luke 8:22-25). He changes water into wine at Cana (John 2:1-11). He feeds a multitude (Mark 6:32-44 , Matt 14:13-21, Luke 9:10-17, John 6:1-15). Of all these stories only the last one, according to Meier, is likely to have some basis in an event of Jesus' life. All the others, he believes, have too many features that argue to creation by the early church for theological purposes.

The feeding of the multitude is the only miracle story recounted (albeit in different versions) by all four gospels. This is especially significant because scholars agree that John's gospel is in its literary ancestry independent of the other three. Moreover, the story coheres with teachings of the historical Jesus that likened the coming kingdom of God to a festive banquet and with the fact that banquets—eating and drinking and table fellowship—are strongly associated with Jesus' public ministry. Jesus' habit of festive suppers culminated in the Last Supper before his crucifixion. All these features lead Meier to the conclusion that these stories recall "some especially memorable communal meal of bread and fish, a meal with eschatological overtones celebrated by Jesus and his disciples with a large crowd by the Sea of Galilee" (v. II, 966). What actually happened at this memorable meal the historian cannot say. Obviously the early church believed that Jesus performed a miracle by making a few loaves of bread and some fish able to feed a large crowd. For our purpose of getting to know the historical Jesus, we have plenty to contemplate with the bare bones of the story as Meier constructs it. Jesus seems to be aware of the eschatological dimensions of this festive meal; that is, he is aware that this activity of a festive meal is both a foretaste and a promise of the future and final kingdom of God and makes that kingdom in some way present. We can ask him to reveal to us his own thoughts, feelings, and reactions during this meal, and especially his sense of the presence of God his Father during the meal.

The early church obviously took the elements of the original story and embellished them with eucharistic references. For example, in Mark 8:6 we read: "He took the seven loaves, and after giving thanks he broke them and gave them to his disciples." Later at the Last Supper we read: "he took a loaf of bread, and after blessing it he broke it, gave it to them" (Mark 14:22). In John's gospel the feeding of the multitude in chapter 6 leads to the great discourse on the bread of life, with clear references to the eucharist. Once again we see how the early church and the writers of the gospels took events in the life of the historical Jesus and embellished them to witness to their faith in Jesus and to evoke faith in their listeners and readers.

Frederick Buechner has written a number of novels about religious figures, but one of the most entertaining and strangely moving is the four-part *Book of Bebb*, four novels about an oddball preacher named Leo Bebb who beggars description. In the third novel, *Love Feast*, Bebb and his friend and benefactor Gertrude Conover decide to invite to Thanksgiving dinner all the Princeton students who have to stay on campus. Only about twenty show up, but there is food for hundreds more. Just before the meal is to start, Bebb gets the attention of the people present and tells them Jesus' parable of the rich man who prepared a big banquet and no one came. He then tells them that they have prepared food for many more and convinces them to go out into the streets of Princeton and invite in anyone they can find.

In an hour or so the house is packed with people. "Young and old, black and white, town and gown—'Antonio, it's Noah's ark,' Bebb said to me at some point. 'We got two of everything, only here it's the clean and unclean both.'" Near the end of the meal Bebb gives a very moving speech. Here are parts of it:

He said, "The Kingdom of Heaven is like a great feast. That's the way of it. The Kingdom of Heaven is a love feast where nobody's a stranger. Like right here. There's strangers everywheres else you can think of. There's strangers born twin brothers out of the same womb. There's strangers was raised together in the same town and worked side by side all their life through. There's strangers got married and been climbing in and out of the same four-poster thirty-five, forty years, and they're strangers still. And Jesus, it's like most of the time he is a stranger too. But here in this place there's no strangers, and Jesus, he isn't a stranger either. The Kingdom of Heaven's like this."

He said, "We all got secrets. I got them same as everybody else—things we feel bad about and wish hadn't ever happened. Hurtful things. Long ago things. We're all scared and lonesome, but most of the time we keep it hid. It's like every one of us has lost his way so bad we don't even know which way is home any more

106

only we're ashamed to ask. You know what would happen if we would own up we're lost and ask? Why, what would happen is we'd find out home is each other. We'd find home is Jesus that loves us lost or found or any whichway. . . .

"Dear hearts," Bebb said, "we got to love one another and Jesus or die guessing." Bebb said, "I wasn't born yesterday. I'm not kidding myself what we got going here is a hundred percent guaranteed to last forever. There's nothing in this world lasts forever. That's the miserable sadness of it. . . . Friends, while we're still sitting here feeling good let us promise to remember how for a little bit of time we loved each other in this place. Even when the party's over, let us remember the good time we had here with Jesus" (56-57).

For all its wackiness I find in this "Love Feast" a novelistic creation of what we all most deeply want and which Jesus' memorable festive meal with the multitude on the shore of the Sea of Galilee might have been like.

We ourselves might use our contemplation of the story of Jesus' festive meal to ask his help to appreciate more deeply the eucharistic mystery. We can become so used to the weekly or even daily celebration of the eucharist that we lose a sense of the awesome mystery of what we profess when we celebrate it. As a result, our experience of the mystery can be greatly attenuated. We might also want to ask Jesus to help us to appreciate his deep desire to see his followers enjoy table fellowship and the sacramental presence of the mystery we call God with everyone, not just with family and friends or people of their own social class or nationality. We might also ask him to help us to desire more strongly the breakdown of the scandalous divisions in the Christian churches which keep us from sharing the eucharist with so many fellow Christians.

Jesus and 5 Discipleship

In this chapter we want to see what we can know about the meaning of discipleship, of following Jesus. After we finish this chapter, we might find it a little more difficult to express this desire to follow Jesus more closely, because we will see more clearly the consequences of doing so.

> *We have begun each chapter with the desire: "I want to know more about you so that I may love you more intensely and walk with you more closely." Let's begin this chapter in similar fashion.*

The "Twelve"

Already chapter 1 noted that Jesus imitated his mentor, John the Baptist, by gathering around him a group of followers, both men and women. There are good arguments for maintaining that there also was a special group, all men, who became known as "the Twelve." We call these men the twelve apostles. Not every scholar agrees that Jesus singled out twelve, but Meier and Brown believe that the evidence, while not definitive, supports this conclusion (cf. Meier, v. II, 628; Brown, "The Twelve and the Apostolate," *NJBC*, 1380, n. 148). It can be argued that Jesus' choice of the specific number twelve was a conscious recognition that his ministry meant a reconstitution of the house of Israel, which was divided into twelve tribes, ten of which had been lost through conquests and forced exiles. Indeed, he is reported to have promised that these twelve "will also sit on twelve thrones, judging the twelve tribes of Israel" (Matt 19:28). Jesus seems to have had in mind the reconstitution of the full people of Israel, that God would intervene decisively to restore the ten lost tribes to the extant tribes of Benjamin and Juda. We need to notice that Jesus does not call eleven to make up with himself the Twelve; Jesus seems to be conscious of having a unique role in the history of his people. Here again there is fruit for contemplative dialogue with Jesus. What did it mean to him to have such a consciousness of being the bearer of something so radically new in the history of his people?

The Meaning of Discipleship

In the gospels, however, we also read of the larger group comprised of those called disciples. What did the call to discipleship mean? Or, perhaps better, can we know what Jesus intended by calling some people to be disciples? In this chapter I shall be basing my statements on a monograph of the German exegete and theologian Martin Hengel, *The Charismatic Leader and his Followers*, as well as on E. P. Sanders's *The Historical Figure of Jesus*. Hengel bases his conclusions on an exegesis of the strange text in Matthew's gospel where discipleship is at issue.

A scribe then approached and said, "Teacher, I will follow you wherever you go." And Jesus said to him, "Foxes have holes, and birds of the air have nests;

but the Son of Man has nowhere to lay his head." Another of his disciples said to him, "Lord, first let me go and bury my father." But Jesus said to him, "Follow me, and let the dead bury their own dead" (Matt 8:19-22).

The strange part of this text is Jesus' last remark. In effect, he puts following him before one of the most sacred duties enjoined on a Jew by the Law and by the interpretations of the Law, namely, to bury the dead, especially to bury one's own dead father. Because Jesus' statement is so contrary to what would be expected of a pious Jew, or for that matter any pious loving son, Hengel argues to its historicity as a saying of Jesus. If Jesus had not so responded, the argument goes, the early church would not have preserved the statement. Moreover, Hengel points out that this is another instance of how Jesus formulated maxims in short, pithy phrases, which tells us something about the kind of person the historical Jesus was. Hengel writes: "The impression we gain is that Jesus is deliberately trying to provoke people by this sharp rejoinder of his; there is indeed a similar tendency to be found in some pronouncements in Qoheleth [Ecclesiastes], whose words were compared by his disciple to 'ox-goads' and to 'nails firmly fixed'" (7).

Beginning with this text Hengel goes on to show that discipleship, in spite of the fact that the word's Latin root refers to learning, did *not* mean becoming a student of Jesus the way young men became students of rabbis. Jesus *peremptorily* called his disciples. Rabbis did not call their students; the students chose them. In addition, Jesus did not call people to follow him as a political revolutionary. Rather, following him meant taking on the same mission Jesus himself had, sharing his itinerant and homeless ministry with all its attendant dangers. Hengel comes to the same conclusion as does Meier about the mission of Jesus, as we can see from this statement:

> In what he did, Jesus' aim was . . . to proclaim the nearness of God in word and deed, to call to repentance, and to proclaim the will of God understood radically in the light of the imminent rule of God, which indeed was already dawning in his activity; similarly, "following after" him and "discipleship" were orientated to this one great aim (53).

Hengel states that Jesus and his disciples most likely lived on donations and made little, if any, provision for the future. "Consequently, 'following after' has primarily the very concrete sense of following him *in his wanderings and sharing with him his uncertain and indeed perilous destiny,* and becoming his pupils only in a derivative sense" (54). Hence Jesus can say to one of those who want to follow him, "Foxes have holes, and birds of the air have nests; but the Son of Man has nowhere to lay his head."

Did Jesus call everyone to this kind of discipleship? Hengel and Sanders argue against this. In view of the coming kingdom of God all were called to repent of their sinful ways, to act mercifully and kindly to others, to forgive their neighbor in response to the unconditional forgiveness offered by God, in short, to love one another. In other words, as Sanders says, Jesus "would have liked everyone to be a supporter, but apparently he intentionally called only a few to *follow* him in the strict sense of the word" (*The Historical Figure of Jesus,* 123). Only particular people were called to give up ties to family and possessions and even to forsake sacred obligations in order to put themselves wholeheartedly at the service of the kingdom of God as Jesus had done. Jesus called these particular people, just as earlier God called Moses and the prophets and brooked no objection. Not everyone was called to give up all ordinary ties to family, occupation, and possessions, but only those whom Jesus, for his own reasons, called. In other words, once again we see Jesus acting in a unique manner, indeed, in a manner reminiscent of God in the Hebrew Bible. We might want to ask him to reveal to us his sense of his identity and what it was like to come to this sense of his own unique relationship with God.

It is clear from the gospels that those called were not religious geniuses, saints, or even people of a particular social class. The first ones called seem to have been fishermen, one of whom, at least, was married (Peter); Jesus is also said to have called as a disciple a tax collector, a man considered to be a cheat; and finally, of course, he called Judas Iscariot. Jesus, argues Hengel, was not setting up a double class of followers, the "unwashed masses" and the "elite." For his own reasons, however, he wanted some people to give up everything to follow him in his total commitment to the kingdom of God. Those who were called were free to accept or reject the call; by rejecting it, they did not lose his love or their place in God's kingdom. But they might, like the rich young man, go away grieving (Mark 10:22).

Following Jesus in this special sense had its rewards. The disciples were close to Jesus, saw him in action, got to know him more intimately. But there was also a cost. Like him, they had nowhere to lay their heads; like him, too, they gave up the security of a regular trade and of an ordinary family life. Moreover, it seems that Jesus himself became estranged from his family. There are indications that he found Nazareth, his small home town, inhospitable, so much so that he wondered that "he could do no deed of power there, except that he laid his hands on a few sick people and cured them. And he was amazed at their unbelief" (Mark 6:5-6).

Since Nazareth was a very small town, perhaps only a village, it is entirely possible that his relatives were among those who lacked belief in him, at least in the beginning. Also in Mark we read: "Then he went home [i.e., to Nazareth]; and the crowd came together again, so that they could not even eat. When his family heard it, they went out to restrain him, for people were saying, 'He has gone out of his mind'" (Mark 3:19-21). There may be a hint of an estrangement from his family in the later section of the same chapter:

> Then his mother and his brothers came; and standing outside, they sent to him and called him. A crowd was sitting around him; and they said to him, "Your mother and your brothers and sisters are outside, asking for you." And he replied, "Who are my mother and my brothers?" And looking at those who sat around him, he said, "Here are my mother and my brothers! Whoever does the will of God is my brother and sister and mother" (Mark 3:31-35).

Did the disciples experience estrangement from their families? One can bet that if the disciple who asked to bury his father obeyed Jesus rather than the command of Law and piety he suffered for it. We might recall another group of sayings that have some claim to having come—at least in some form—from the lips of the historical Jesus:

> "I came to bring fire to the earth, and how I wish it were already kindled! I have a baptism with which to be baptized, and what stress I am under until it is completed! Do you think that I have come to bring peace to the earth? No, I tell you, but rather division! From now on five in one household will be divided, three against two and two against three; they will be divided: father against son and son against father, mother against daughter and daughter against mother, mother-in-law against her daughter-in-law and daughter-in-law against mother-in-law" (Luke 12:49-53).

There is certainly food for thought and for dialogue with Jesus in these reflections about discipleship. How did he react to the estrangement from his own family? How did he feel about making such demands on some of his followers? How do I react to the fact that he chose some people out of the crowds around him to be followers in this special sense? Is there elitism in his choices? How do I feel now about the desire to follow Jesus more closely?

Jesus and Women Followers

Women belonged to the circle around Jesus, even though it is not clear whether they were called disciples in the technical sense we have just examined. Martin Hengel says the fact that women belonged to his circle "is completely incompatible with understanding him (Jesus) as a teacher like the rabbis (since only men could be students of Torah in Jesus' days), but is logically in line with Jesus' turning towards the weak and

the despised: the sinners, the sick and the children"
(74). The fact that women seem to have played significant roles in the church of New Testament times (see
Elizabeth Schüssler-Fiorenza, *In Memory of Her*) indicates that Jesus' own policy with regard to women was
a strong counterweight to the patriarchal ethos of the
time. Again we can find food for our contemplative
conversation with Jesus here.

Women did play key roles in the gospels. For one
thing, Jesus received financial support from women. In
Luke we read:

> The twelve were with him, as well as some women
> who had been cured of evil spirits and infirmities:
> Mary, called Magdalene, from whom seven demons
> had gone out, and Joanna, the wife of Herod's stew-
> ard Chuza, and Susanna, and many others, who pro-
> vided for them out of their resources (Luke 8:1-3).

In Mark we read that women stayed with Jesus
through the crucifixion: "There were also women looking on from a distance; among them were Mary Magdalene, and Mary the mother of James the younger and
of Joses, and Salome." Mark makes no mention of Jesus' male followers being at the scene. The writer goes
on to say: "These [women] used to follow him and provided for him when he was in Galilee; and there were
many other women who had come up with him to
Jerusalem" (Mark 15:40-41). Women also became the
first witnesses of the resurrected Jesus. Sanders notes:

> It is hard to be sure of their importance to Jesus dur-
> ing his lifetime, but I think that their support was
> significant. . . . It was presumably these women who
> joined with the disciples in prayer in the upper room,

116

before Peter's first sermon (Acts 1:14). We do not know anything else about them: history was then, as for centuries before and after, the history of males, and for the most part women play only supporting roles. For this one brief period, crucial to Christianity, Jesus' women followers are in the limelight (*The Historical Figure of Jesus*, 125).

A conversation with Jesus about his attitudes toward women might prove very fruitful.

In our day, obviously, the question of the role of women in the church has taken on great significance and been a source of both pain and joy. I have known faithful and devoted Christian women who believe in their bones that they have been called to follow Jesus as disciples as closely as any man. I have also been spiritual director of and ministerial collaborator with a number of Roman Catholic women who believe that they were called to ministerial priesthood. Some of them have said that at first they did not trust the authenticity of the call since it seemed so impossible of fulfillment; when they doubted the authenticity of the call, however, they felt a deterioration in their relationship with Jesus. These women have not become bitter because their call could not be fulfilled; they have remained at peace and continued to minister as best they could. But they cannot honestly say that their call to ministerial priesthood is a delusion and still be true to themselves or to their relationship with Jesus.

Discipleship Today

In the gospels Jesus is depicted as sending out the twelve on mission. "Then Jesus called the twelve together and gave them power and authority over all demons and to cure diseases, and he sent them out to proclaim the kingdom of God and to heal" (Luke 9:1-2). At another time he is said to have sent out "seventy others," again with the mission to heal and to proclaim the kingdom of God. They have the same mission as Jesus, an urgent one in view of the fact that Jesus believed that the kingdom of God was imminent. That Jesus did use these followers to enhance his own mission, it is argued, is historical. Throughout history men and women have felt themselves called to give up all familial and cultural ties to be on mission with Jesus. This sense of a call continues today. In my experience those who have the conviction of such a call do not think of themselves as better than other Christians; rather, they marvel at the fact that they have been called, resist believing in it, and are immensely grateful when they accept it.

I recall a time when I engaged in a discussion with some other Jesuits about the merits of the vow of chastity. I became more and more uneasy with the arguments for the vow that seemed to me to be too utilitarian; for example, that the vow of chastity makes a person more available for mission. Finally I blurted out something like this: "I'm a Jesuit because God wants my happiness, because being a Jesuit is the best way for me to be fulfilled, and God knows that." I surprised myself actually, but now, thirty-five years later, I still feel the same way. I am very grateful that I have been called, and I can give no good arguments about my utility to Jesus or God. Jesus does not need me, but I am very happy that he wants me as his disciple.

By the way, I am not arguing that chastity is a necessary part of the call to radical discipleship; after all, a number of the closest disciples were married. Many married couples have, in our day, felt the radical call to discipleship, have sold all that they had, and followed Jesus. In a short memoir about her sister Toni, who died of cancer, Martha Gies notes that Toni and her husband Eugene signed on with Wycliffe Bible Translators to go to the Peruvian jungle as temporary missionaries and took their two children. "After four and a half months in Peru, Toni and Eugene decided to be missionaries for real. Their plan was to come home, liquidate their few assets, raise the money for their ministry, and sign on for a long term program" (Martha Gies, "A Heart of Wisdom," 12). Sickness intervened to prevent the carrying out of their intention.

I take comfort when I realize that the ones Jesus chose as his disciples in his lifetime were neither heroes nor saints. The gospel of Mark paints a rather dim picture of the Twelve; no matter how hard Jesus tries to get them to see the kingdom from his (and God's) point of view, they are blind, as I noted in the last chapter when speaking of the cure of the two blind men in Mark. One of the twelve betrays him to the Jewish authorities; Peter, in cowardly fashion, three times denies knowing Jesus; and all of them run away. It may be comforting to know that Jesus did not choose "winners" as his closest friends.

There is some indication that in calling people to discipleship Jesus did not demand that they fulfill all the obligations of the Law to show repentance and thus be brought back into the people of God. A tax collector, for example, in order to be reconciled with God and God's people, was expected to make restitution to those whom he had cheated, pay a fine of 20 percent of the ill-gotten gain, and sacrifice a ram as a guilt offering. There is no indication that Jesus demanded that Levi fulfill these obligations before Jesus entered his house for a feast; and while Zacchaeus does spontaneously offer to make restitution, and abundantly, he makes the offer only *after* Jesus has entered his house and eaten with him, causing grumbling among some of the onlookers (cf. Luke 19:1-10). It appears that Jesus ate with the wicked and called sinful people to follow him prior to their having fulfilled the duties of repentance. It is as if he expected that they would change their sinful ways through regular contact with him. Obviously this did not work with Judas Iscariot. Moreover, Jesus expected the rule of God to come at any moment, and his message was, to sinner and saint alike, "God loves you." He backed up this statement by sharing table fellowship with all.

During his lifetime Jesus seems to have had a tremendous attractive power. Men and women followed him in his itinerant and marginal ministry. He called some to a radical following, and some of these responded with all their hearts, even if their hearts were weak and vacillating. Down the centuries he has continued to exercise this tremendous attraction, and men and women have heeded what they took as his command—"Follow me!" Do I hear that call? Do I want to hear it?

Recently I read a very moving story, a novelistic treatment of two real Jesuit priests, both of whom, before joining Alcoholics Anonymous, came close to destroying their lives through the abuse of alcohol. The book is called *Anonymous Disciple* and is authored by Gerard Goggins. The main character, given the name

Father Jim Collins, had always thought of himself as made for higher things, "Top Shelf Collins." In the last eighteen years of his life he found happiness and even incredible joy in the fellowship of A.A., especially with broken people. He became a Pied Piper who attracted all kinds of people. He met Kathleen when she was in the locked ward at Worcester State Hospital. Gradually she began to improve through membership in A.A. One evening at a meeting she came up to Jim after another of his broken friends has just finished speaking with him. The following moving scene occurs.

"He's [the man who had just walked away from Fr. Jim] like most of the people in my life. He makes me feel like I should go crawl under a rug," she said. "He despises me. Most people despise me. Everybody despises me. My father despises me. My family despises me. They don't want to have anything to do with me. Sometimes I think God despises me. You know that, Father?"

"I don't despise you," Jim said.

"Yeah. But you're different," Kathleen said. "It's your job. I mean, I'm just part of your quota."

"My what?"

"Your quota. You know. Yeah. Your quota."

"What quota?"

"You know. For lost sheep. That quota. Don't you have a quota? I mean, don't the Jesuits give you a quota?"

Jim wondered if there was a full moon. He looked out the window, but all he could see was the dark outline of a building across the alley.

"Kathleen, some Jesuits don't even speak to me. They think I'm a bum. They're afraid to let me teach. They lock the liquor cabinet when they see me coming. They think I'm a disgrace to the Society. They have no idea what I do at A.A. and they don't care."

"Then what are you doing here?"

Jim seemed puzzled.

"I mean, if they didn't send you, you know, what are you doing here?"

"I'm a drunk. If I want to stay sober, I have to come to A.A.," Jim said.

"But what about me? You know. How come you bought me those clothes? Why do you hang around with me? I mean, if I'm not part of a quota . . ."

"Kathleen," Jim said, "You're my friend. I love you."

"What?" She seemed surprised, almost shocked.

"I love you," Jim said. "I enjoy your company. I like being with you."

Kathleen's exterior shell had cracked. She seemed very vulnerable. "Me? Are you crazy? Nobody loves me." She was on the verge of tears. "Why?" she asked.

"Because you're lovable," Jim replied.

As Kathleen turned to walk away, she began to cry. . . .

As the meeting hall was emptying, Kathleen tugged on Father Jim's sleeve.

"Did you really mean what you said?" she asked.

"Of course," he said.

"Well I've been thinking, then. You know. I mean if you love— I mean if some human being actually loves me—if you love me—and you're not kidding— and I'm not part of some Jesuit quota for finding lost sheep—if you really love me, just because, well, just because you love me—just because I'm me—then maybe, Father—I mean maybe—then it's possible— that God loves me?"

122

"Of course God loves you. You're the apple of his eye. He's nuts about you."

"Really, Father?" Kathleen asked with a big smile.

"Really," Jim said.

"I could float," Kathleen said. "I could just float right out of here."

Later in the story when Jim is hospitalized for one of his numerous illnesses, he and the other Jesuit, Fred, are talking late at night. Jim, the talkative one, engages in this soliloquy:

"Sometimes I look back at it and I wonder. I wonder if I missed my calling, if the bus I was supposed to be on pulled out and I was left standing on the curb.

"All my friends are broken people. Even you, Fred, my best friend, are broken. You're not as broken as you were. Remember how your head used to shake?

"I thought that my friends would all be great minds, doers of great projects, that I would move in the circle of the elite. And here I am an old man with a broken body, addicted to cigarettes, and all of my friends are broken people. There isn't a great composer or a great writer or a great poet—at least that I know of—among them.

"You think of the great mystics. St. Teresa and John of the Cross. All the great saints who had such a personal and intimate relationship with Christ, and here I am getting only a glimpse now and then—just occasionally spotting his shadow a second after he turns the corner ahead of me.

"One night, years ago, as I was falling asleep, I heard his voice. I thought it was someone out in the hall. I can still remember it. 'Visit the sick. Comfort the afflicted. Heal the brokenhearted,' he said. And

'Follow me.' and I guess that's what we were doing when you went into the prisons and I went into the hospitals. Maybe you realized it, but I didn't. I just went. You suggested it. I wasn't even sure of what I was doing. Sometimes I wasn't even sure that He was with me. And I wound up receiving all these gifts, these wonderful broken people who turned out to be my friends. Kathleen, ah Fred, Kathleen. And Bobby with his impetuousness and his dreams of glory. And Anthony. Who would have expected Anthony to become such a power of example?

"And I think of what Peter asked him. 'What about us who have put aside everything to follow you?' And he said you will receive it back a hundred fold just in this life alone, never mind the one to come. And I have, Fred. I have received the hundred fold."

Later as Fred was about to leave, Jim said:

"You know, we are blessed."

Fred nodded.

"I wonder what kind of man I would be if I was not an alcoholic. I wonder what kind of Jesuit. I'd probably be proud and off the track. I'd have wound up being an apostate or a ladies man. I would have been a disgrace to the Society. And instead, because I'm an alcoholic and because of A.A. and because of you, Fred, I have found love and peace and fulfillment. I have found friendship, and I have found my vocation even if it's not the one I expected."

Fred nodded. "Goodnight, Jim."

"It's God that did it to us, Fred."

"I know."

124

Jesus' 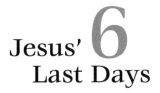6
Last Days

We come now to the final week of Jesus' life on earth.

> *Again we express our desire: "I want to know more about you so that I may love you more intensely and walk with you more closely." Perhaps the desire now can be even more focused: "May I have an interior knowledge of what Jesus went through during this last week of his life on earth."*

Date and Background

Most likely in the spring of 30 A.D. (or perhaps 33 A.D.) Jesus journeyed with his disciples from Galilee to Jerusalem for the feast of Passover. (Meier argues that Jesus' public ministry lasted two years and a couple of months; see v. I, 406). Passover (or Unleavened Bread) began on the fifteenth day of the Jewish month Nisan (March-April) and lasted for eight days. It was a pilgrim feast; all male Jews theoretically were obliged to go to Jerusalem, if possible. Hence, large crowds flowed from the various towns and villages of Galilee and Judea and beyond toward Jerusalem. The usual custom was to come a week early in order to purify and prepare oneself for the celebration of the feast days.

This is probably why Jesus and his disciples arrived the week before Passover.

Because of the large crowds, Roman and Jewish authorities took extra precautions to forestall a riot or an uprising. Hence, the Roman prefect came from Caesarea to Jerusalem with extra troops. At the time of Jesus' ministry Pontius Pilate was prefect.

It is possible that on this journey to Jerusalem, which turned out to be his last, Jesus cured the blind Bartimaeus on the outskirts of Jericho and that he uttered the plaintive words about Jerusalem we read in Luke 13:34-35:

> "Jerusalem, Jerusalem, the city that kills the prophets and stones those who are sent to it! How often have I desired to gather your children together as a hen gathers her brood under her wings, and you were not willing! See, your house is left to you. And I tell you, you will not see me until the time comes when you say, 'Blessed is the one who comes in the name of the Lord.'"

Did Jesus have at least a foreboding that this journey would be a fateful one for him and for his people? We shall see the evidence for this surmise later.

It might be a good idea at this point to ask ourselves what we know about the historical Jesus' own sense of identity. We have seen that he must have been conscious of himself as a prophet in the line of the great prophets of the past, if not even a greater one. In addition, he seems to have been conscious of having a very special relationship with God, whom he called Abba, "my own dear Father." He seems to have believed that with his life and ministry a decisive time for his people and perhaps for the world had arrived, the fulfillment of God's promise to come to rule the world with justice. He viewed himself as a worker of wonders, wonders which announced that the kingdom of God had indeed come very close. He seems to have believed that he had the warrant to interpret the Law authoritatively and to call disciples in as peremptory a manner as God called prophets and leaders in earlier times. He was considered the Messiah by at least some of his followers, but he himself was leery of this title, perhaps because he knew that he could not fulfill the expectations of the Messiah commonly held by his fellow Jews. It is not clear that he used the title Son of God of himself, but Meier thinks it a possibility. He seems to have preferred the title Son of Man, but it is not easy to know what he meant by the title. Meier believes that "Jesus the parable maker used the enigmatic, parablelike designation Son of Man to refer in a paradoxical way to himself as the lowly, disreputable messenger of the powerful kingdom of God" (Meier, "Jesus," *NJBC*, 1325, n. 39). One of the reasons he was abhorred by some Jewish authorities seems to have been that he had an exalted sense of his own identity vis-a-vis God. In fact, his actions and words could easily be considered blasphemous by any pious Jew, even if he never explicitly said that he was Son of God, that is, that he was equal to God.

At any rate, as he approached Jerusalem for what would be his last time, he carried with him from Galilee a sense of his identity and mission and a reputation for being a wonder worker, considered by some as the Messiah. Moreover, he had earned the strong opposition of some of the leading Jews of Galilee. According to his own words, recorded in Matthew, he had experienced wholesale rejection in a number of towns of Galilee.

> Then he began to reproach the cities in which most of his deeds of power had been done, because they did not repent. "Woe to you, Chorazin! Woe to you, Bethsaida! For if the deeds of power done in you had been done in Tyre and Sidon, they would have repented long ago in sackcloth and ashes. But I tell you, on the day of judgment it will be more tolerable for Tyre and Sidon than for you. And you, Capernaum, will you be exalted to heaven? No, you will be brought down to Hades. For if the deeds of power done in you had been done in Sodom, it would have remained until this day. But I tell you that on the day of judgment it will be more tolerable for the land of Sodom than for you" (Matt 11:20-24).

Apparently, he had aroused a good deal of hostility during his ministry in Galilee. It also seems that he did not trim his sails to the wind of this hostility. Against this background he now comes up to Jerusalem with the great crowds of other pilgrims, many of whom had probably heard of him. Since the high priest was held responsible by the Roman prefect for good order during these festivals, he and those around him might have been more than a little skittish as this festival approached. Once again Jesus did not trim his sails, even though he was aware of the growing opposition to him.

Entry into Jerusalem

Jesus began his last week in such a dramatic fashion that it probably tipped the scales toward his arrest and execution. Both Sanders and Meier tend to believe that Jesus did ride into Jerusalem on a donkey, a symbolic act referring to the prophecy of Zechariah. If he did so, and even if the event was not as spectacular as depicted in the gospels, he apparently made a symbolic assertion that he was indeed a "king," or the Messiah, as he entered David's city. Even if the outpouring of adulation was less dramatic than the gospels depict, the event would nonetheless have made the high priest and his entourage nervous just prior to the Holy Days.

Meier and others also believe that Jesus performed another symbolic act at this time, namely the cleansing of the Temple (cf. Mark 11:15-17). While it is difficult to know what Jesus intended with this action, it would again have disturbed the high priest and other Jewish authorities. According to Meier, Jesus could have been claiming authority over how Temple business should be conducted, in itself a striking and daring claim not calculated to endear him to the Temple authorities. But he could also have been making an even more ominous claim—that the Temple would be destroyed. The main charge brought against him at the trial before the high priest, after all, was that he threatened to destroy the Temple. Sanders argues for this intention since Jesus often spoke of the new order that would come with God's kingdom, which was imminent. For Jesus, the coming destruction would not be the work of Jewish revolutionaries or of foreign armies, but of God. Jesus did not seem much interested in politics at any time in his life; his central message, as we have seen many times, was that God was about to act to bring about the kingdom of God.

Meier sums up his interpretation of the triumphal entry and the cleansing of the Temple thus:

These two symbolic actions of Jesus the prophet, actions redolent of the OT prophets, may have been the reasons why the priestly aristocracy chose to strike at Jesus during this particular visit to Jerusalem, as opposed to his earlier stays. Thus, Jesus himself had chosen to press the issue, forcing the capital of Israel to make a decision for or against him, the final prophet of its history (Meier, "Jesus," NJBC, 1326, n. 44).

Clearly these symbolic actions are of a piece with what we have already conjectured about Jesus' sense of his identity and mission. We can spend some time in prayer asking Jesus to enlighten us about his motives and his hopes. What were his feelings, his dreams, his foreboding during this climactic and dramatic entry into the Holy City?

In the gospels Jesus is depicted as knowing that he would die a violent death, and indeed that he would die by crucifixion. Since the gospels were written long after the actual crucifixion, it is difficult to know how much of these prophecies of his crucifixion are directly from Jesus and how much from the early church. Given the opposition that he had been arousing, Jesus must have had premonitions about meeting a violent death. He saw himself as a prophet of the end times, and in his lifetime such prophets were viewed as martyrs. Jesus himself is reported to have said: "Jerusalem, Jerusalem, the city that kills the prophets and stones those who are sent to it!" (Matt 23:37). Moreover he had seen what had befallen John the Baptist as a result of his ministry. Jesus must have been aware of the possibility of his own martyrdom. In spite of this he performed these two symbolic actions, which probably sealed his doom.

The Last Supper

There is confusion in the gospels about the exact date of the Last Supper and whether it was the Passover meal. Meier (in v. I) argues for the historical accuracy of the gospel of John's chronology; namely, that the Last Supper was not a Passover meal, but was held on the evening before Passover. His position is this: Jesus sensed that his enemies were getting ready for a final attack on him and perhaps that one of his own disciples was in league with them; hence he decided to celebrate a final meal with his closest disciples, using a room provided by one of his supporters who lived in Jerusalem. During this meal he used bread and wine to symbolize his imminent death. Meier states: "Jesus' words ran something like this, 'This is my flesh [body],' and 'This [cup?] is [= contains, mediates] the covenant [sealed] by my blood.' . . . Jesus therefore interpreted his death as the . . . means by which God would restore the covenant with Israel at Sinai" ("Jesus," *NJBC*, 1327, n. 51). Thus, Jesus was aware that this would be his last supper with his closest disciples. Meier concludes: "This last meal was a pledge that, despite the apparent failure of his mission, God would vindicate Jesus even beyond death and bring him and his followers to the eschatological banquet" (Ibid.).

As we ponder these words and actions at the Last Supper, we might ask Jesus to let us know his attitude toward death, toward his Abba, and toward his mission. What kind of person could contemplate with such apparent equanimity the complete failure of his mission? Throughout his public ministry he had preached complete trust in God, who would vindicate the people and even overcome death itself. As we contemplate these events of his last night on earth, we see that he kept this filial faith and trust to the end. It is presumed that Judas was one of the close disciples who celebrated this final meal with Jesus. We might also want Jesus to reveal to us his attitude toward Judas Iscariot, his betrayer.

Down the centuries since this Last Supper Christians have commemorated Jesus' last meal as the eucharist, which means "giving thanks." In eating the consecrated bread and drinking the consecrated wine, we believe that we participate in the death and resurrection of Jesus. Often enough, I suppose, we have felt no sensible consolation in receiving the eucharist; but occasionally God breaks through the routine, and we are touched deeply by the knowledge that we are indeed participating in the death and resurrection of Jesus in a special way. As we contemplate the historical Jesus' last meal, we might recall such significant moments and ask for the grace to be more mindful of the great mystery that is the eucharist.

Reynolds Price provides an example of what the eucharist can mean in special circumstances. He had just finished the second series of radiation treatments for the tumor in his spinal cord and confronted the fact that he might never walk again. In a black mood he looked up to the ceiling of his bedroom and asked God, "How much more do I take?" After a long silent pause he heard a voice say, "More." He interpreted this to mean that he would not have ease yet. The next morning he asked a friend to have her Methodist minister bring him the sacrament of communion. He then recalls the aftermath of receiving the eucharist:

> Since my first taste in childhood of the meager portions of bread and wine . . . I'd been a natural believer

in the actual presence of Jesus in the swallowed fragments. Unlike Roman Catholics, I felt no need to sense the elements as literal human flesh and blood; but perhaps as intensely as any mystic, in the slow eating that one morning, I experienced again the almost overwhelming force which has always felt to me like God's presence. Whether the force would confirm my healing or go on devastating me, for the moment I barely cared. No prior taste in my old life had meant as much as this new chance at a washed and clarified view of my fate—and that from the hands of a strange minister in a room which didn't belong to me. In many calmer hours to come, I'd know that my answer to the one word More was three words anyhow— Bring it on (*A Whole New Life,* 81-82).

Perhaps reading this experience will help recall times when the eucharist was a special experience. Mind you, the special times occur against the backdrop of ordinary experiences of the eucharist, which in mysterious ways are also profound meetings with Jesus.

Arrest and Trials

At the end of the supper Jesus and the disciples went to the garden of Gethsemane, a name that means "oil press" or "oil vat", at the foot of the Mount of Olives. Brown posits "that early Christians had a tradition that before he died Jesus struggled in prayer about his fate" (*The Death of the Messiah,* v. I, 225). Though we may not know what Jesus' exact words were, the early Christians believed that he was in agony as he prayed and that he finally surrendered in faith and trust to his Abba. Jesus was in his early thirties, the prime of his life. He sensed the shipwreck of all his hopes and of his ministry. We can ask him to help us to empathize with him in these final hours.

As Jesus was praying, Judas led an armed band there. Did Judas betray Jesus with a kiss? After looking at all the evidence and all the opinions Brown says that there is no way to establish the historical truth (Ibid., 255). Jesus refused to use force to evade arrest and was taken prisoner. The gospels depict the disciples as fleeing in terror. This detail would hardly have been invented by the early church; hence it is regarded as historical. Jesus was left alone to face his fate.

It is difficult to reconstruct what happened between Jesus' arrest and the trial before the Roman prefect, Pontius Pilate. Most likely there was a hearing or some kind of trial before the Temple authorities. At this trial religious accusations were brought against Jesus, which, as Meier says, "could probably have been summed up under the vague label of blasphemy, broadly understood" ("Jesus," NJBC, 1327, n. 53). Jesus was not arrested and condemned, according to Meier, for any one reason. It was probably the cumulative effect of what he had done and said during his public ministry that led Caiaphas and the other religious authorities of Jerusalem to see him as a serious danger to peaceful coexistence between them and the Romans.

In our contemplation of the historical Jesus we undoubtedly have become aware of this cumulative effect. Jesus preached the imminent coming of God's kingdom which would write *finis* to the present state of affairs in Israel and, perhaps, in the world. He taught with authority about God's will even when his teaching went contrary to some authoritative interpretations of the Mosaic Law. Perhaps by choosing the Twelve he made a symbolic gesture of restoring the twelve tribes of Israel. He shared table fellowship with tax collectors and the wicked and did not demand that they first be reconciled in the manner prescribed by the Law and its interpretation. He healed the sick and raised the dead and in doing so indicated that in some fashion God's kingdom was already present in his ministry. With all of this he was attracting large crowds. Finally, as Meier says, with the triumphal entry into Jerusalem and the cleansing of the Temple "we have the match set to the barrel of gasoline" (v. II, 628).

Caiaphas and those around him decided that Jesus had to be silenced. The statement attributed to Caiaphas in John's gospel gives at least a hint of the psychology of Caiaphas, who had to work closely with the Roman prefect to prevent riots that might bring down the might of Rome on Israel: "You do not understand that it is better for you to have one man die for the people than to have the whole nation destroyed" (11:50). Given all that we have seen of the historical Jesus, it is not difficult to imagine the charge of blasphemy (broadly understood) being laid against him.

Some questions that might aid contemplation: How did Jesus react to the betrayal by Judas, to his arrest, and to the trial before Caiaphas? How did he react to the charges brought against him and to his condemnation by leaders of his own religion? Another point that is considered historically true is the denial by Peter. It is difficult to see why the early church would have made up this story about its leader. How did Jesus react to Peter's denial? Given the later history of Peter in the early church, we have to say that somehow or other Jesus conveyed his forgiveness to Peter.

Apparently the Temple authorities did not have the right to put a person to death, but they did have recourse to Pilate. But Pilate, however, was not interested in religious charges. Hence, argues Meier, the chief priest and his entourage translated the religious charge of blasphemy into a political one—that Jesus claimed to be "king of the Jews." This title was hung on the cross as the reason for his crucifixion. Sanders believes that the stories about Pilate's hesitations and attempts to let Jesus off with just a scourging are later additions of the Christian community. His argument is that the Christian community would have wanted to mitigate the role of Roman authorities in the death of Jesus in order to lessen suspicious about their religion among present Roman authorities. In reality, Pilate was known as a prefect who had few qualms in ordering executions; in fact, he was removed from his post for indiscriminate executions. "Pilate was a high-handed, stern ruler who never went out of his way to ingratiate himself with the Jews. Writing to Caligula, Herod Agrippa I described Pilate as 'inflexible by nature and cruel because of stubbornness' and accused him of 'graft, insults, robberies, assaults, wanton abuse, constant executions without trial, unending grievous cruelty'" (Fitzmyer, "From Pompey to Bar Cochba," *NJBC*, 1249, n. 168). Hence, Sanders believes that Pilate ordered Jesus crucified rather quickly and without any trial at all.

The Crucifixion and Death

Prisoners sentenced to execution were routinely scourged, a cruel punishment but one that did hasten death. Jesus was so weakened by the ordeals he had suffered and the scourging that he could not carry his own crossbeam. Hence, Simon from Cyrene was pressed into service. (Later he and his sons may have become notable figures in the early Jerusalem church [see Mark 15:21].)

Crucifixion was a remarkably cruel and painful way to die. Brown believes that Jesus was nailed to the cross through the wrists and probably through the feet. One can easily imagine the pain inflicted by such a procedure. The fact that Jesus died so quickly indicates that his body was not given any supports that would make the dying last longer (Brown, *The Death of the Messiah*, 945-52). As he hung on the cross, Jesus was reviled by passersby. In addition to Simon, says Meier, the only other sympathetic witnesses were some of his women followers ("Jesus," *NJBC*, 1328, n. 55). Jesus was crucified with two bandits.

Because these crucifixions took place on the preparation day for the Passover, which coincided with the sabbath, the deaths were hastened so the bodies could be taken down and buried and thus not defile the sabbath. The two bandits had their legs broken to hasten their death, but Jesus died before that measure had to be taken in his regard.

Jesus would have been buried in a pauper's grave except for the intervention of Joseph of Arimathea, who got permission to bury him hastily in a tomb nearby which he owned. The women took note of where he was buried with the intention of coming back after the sabbath to take care of the burial rituals. Mary Magdalene is mentioned both as a witness of the crucifixion and of the hasty burial. (For these details see Meier "Jesus," *NJBC*, 1328, 55-56.)

Down through the centuries Christians have contemplated this scene, sometimes horrified at the enormity of what human beings did to God's best gift to us, sometimes overwhelmed with gratitude that Jesus remained true to his mission to the end, sometimes overcome with grief for what he suffered. Often enough such contemplation leads to the realization that Jesus still suffers crucifixion when his followers suffer persecution and injustice and death. Contemplation of this scene often leads to a wider sympathy for the suffering of others, especially the "little ones" of this world, and to a willingness to stand up for them even under the threat of punishment or death. Oscar Romero, the martyred Archbishop of San Salvador, is an example. In an interview just two weeks before he was assassinated while celebrating Mass he said:

> I have frequently been threatened with death. I must say that, as a Christian, I do not believe in death but in the resurrection. If they kill me, I will rise again in the people of El Salvador. I am not boasting; I say it with the greatest humility. As a pastor, I am bound by divine command to give my life for those whom I love, and that includes all Salvadorans, even those who are going to kill me. . . . I shall be offering my blood for the redemption and resurrection of El Salvador. Martyrdom is a grace from God that I do not believe that I have earned. . . . May my death, if it is accepted by God, be for the liberation of my people. . . . You can tell them, if they succeed in killing me, that I pardon them. . . . But I wish that they could realize that they are wasting their time. A bishop will die, but the church of God—the people—will never die (quoted in David Gill, "Making Sense of Martyrdom," Human Development, Fall 1991).

The consequence of asking to know Jesus in order to love him and to follow him more closely may be that we become like Jesus, so trusting in the love of God that we are not hindered by fear from speaking the truth, even when it is dangerous to our health and life.

The contemplation of Jesus' passion and compassion for him can also come upon a person almost unbidden, as the following incident recounted by Susan DiGiacomo indicates. She had been diagnosed with Hodgkin's Disease and was facing an operation to remove a tumor attached to her heart and a year of intensive chemotherapy. She had been raised a Catholic but had not been practicing for some time. She found out about the operation and the chemotherapy during Holy Week. Here is the experience she recounts:

On the cool and rainy Holy Thursday afternoon of that week, I was home alone. A classical music program on the radio was playing Orlando di Lasso's "Seven Last Words of Christ." Renaissance polyphony moves me as few other kinds of music do, but that day, staring out the window into the leaden sky as tears ran down my cheeks, I found myself, to my own astonishment, praying with the music in Christ's words as he waited in Gethsemane for the soldiers to come and seize him: "Father, if it be possible, take this cup from me; yet let not my will, but Thine be done."

The meaning of Christ's agony in the garden had always eluded me. It just didn't seem to square with the fearless and heroic Christ my Sunday school teachers wanted us to revere and imitate. Now I saw him as a young man, at thirty-three just my age, facing certain torture and death, and I understood his pain because it had something to do with my own. The apostles had accompanied Christ to the garden, but as the hour grew late, the eleven men who loved him most fell asleep around him. So too was I surrounded by people who loved me but were powerless to stop what was going to happen to me. Like Christ, I was— metaphorically—on my knees, sweating blood, praying for either deliverance or grace, and facing my ordeal alone ("The Case: A Narrative Deconstruction of 'Diagnostic Delay,'" 33-34).

This young woman was given the spirit of compassion, and in the process came to look upon her cancer as a gift because it gave her back her God and Jesus, but also taught her the difficult lesson that all of us must learn; namely, that "everyone 'possesses nothing certainly save a brief loan of his own body.'" I am reminded of the men and woman with HIV/AIDS mentioned in the chapter on Jesus' healing who have come to similar conclusions about their illness as gift.

"He Is 7
Risen!"

As we know, the gospels do not end with the death and burial of Jesus. They proclaim the unexpected good news that Jesus of Nazareth has been raised by God to a new and glorious life. Jesus' closest followers attest to the fact that his tomb was empty and that they experienced Jesus in his glorified resurrected state. Upon their testimony rests our faith in the resurrection of Jesus.

As we rejoice in this good news, we express again our desire; "I want to know more about you so that I may love you more intensely and walk with you more closely."

Jesus' followers testify that the Jesus they experienced after his death was the same Jesus of Nazareth they had followed, the one who had been so cruelly put to death. The earliest written account of witnesses to the resurrection of Jesus is contained in Paul's First Letter to the Corinthians, probably written in the spring of 54 A.D. (Murphy-O'Connor, "The First Letter to the Corinthians," *NJBC*, 799, n. 8):

Now I would remind you, brothers and sisters, of the good news that I proclaimed to you, which you in turn received, in which also you stand, through

141

which also you are being saved, if you hold firmly to the message that I proclaimed to you—unless you have come to believe in vain. For I handed on to you as of first importance what I in turn had received: that Christ died for our sins in accordance with the scriptures, and that he was buried, and that he was raised on the third day in accordance with the scriptures, and that he appeared to Cephas, then to the twelve. Then he appeared to more than five hundred brothers and sisters at one time, most of whom are still alive, though some have died. Then he appeared to James, then to all the apostles. Last of all, as to one untimely born, he appeared also to me. For I am the least of the apostles, unfit to be called an apostle, because I persecuted the church of God (1 Cor 15:1-9).

Paul here hands on a tradition that he himself received, a tradition that "almost certainly originated in a Palestinian community" (Ibid., 812, n. 66). This tradition says that a number of close followers of Jesus, people who probably had been devastated by his crucifixion, affirmed that they had indeed experienced him as alive, mysteriously "raised" from the dead. Paul's reference to his own experience of the risen Christ recounts something that happened to him, probably around 35 A.D., just a few years after the crucifixion of Jesus.

No one claims to have seen what actually happened to the body of Jesus. Eye witnesses are named who attest that the tomb was empty: Peter and the other disciple (John 20:6-8), Mary Magdalene (John 20:11-12), Mary Magdalene and other women (Mark 16:4-6; Luke 24:2-3). The empty tomb tradition has good warrant. Not even the enemies of the Christians denied it; in fact, they took it so much for granted that they explained it by claiming that the body of Jesus had been stolen. What actually happened to the body in the tomb is wrapped in the mystery of God's action.

From the stories of his appearances we sense that the risen Jesus was different from the earthly Jesus. Resurrection did not mean a mere resuscitation of the dead body of Jesus. The stories of resurrection appearances almost universally begin with those to whom he appears not recognizing him immediately. But some gesture or word convinces them that they are experiencing the risen Jesus of Nazareth. For example, Mary only recognizes the "gardener" as Jesus when he says her name (John 20:11-18), and the two disciples on the way to Emmaus finally know him "in the breaking of the bread" (Luke 24:13-35).

Sanders writes: "That Jesus' followers (and later Paul) had resurrection experiences is, in my judgment, a fact. What the reality was that gave rise to the experiences I do not know" (*The Historical Figure of Jesus*, 280). The historian can only go so far. However, even the historian can know that these resurrection experiences transformed the disciples, many of whom had been quite timorous and cowardly, so much that they boldly preached about Jesus, proclaimed his resurrection, in many cases lost their lives because of their faith, and started a movement that has affected all subsequent history. The first chapters of the Acts of the Apostles testify to this transformation. One example alone may suffice to signify their change. The apostles were brought before the council in Jerusalem, which "had them flogged. Then they ordered them not to speak in the name of Jesus, and let them go. As they left the council, they rejoiced that they were considered worthy to suffer dishonor for the sake of the name. And every day in the temple and at home they did not cease to teach and proclaim Jesus as the Messiah" (Acts 5:40-42). Something extraordinary indeed happened to these men and women.

It is to this same risen Jesus that we relate now. This risen Jesus is also Jesus of Nazareth, and he bears in his risen body, mind, and heart all that went into making him the human being he will always be. We Christians believe that Jesus of Nazareth and the risen Jesus are one and the same person. We go further; we affirm that Jesus of Nazareth, who is now risen from the dead, is one with God, the only Son of God, the Word made flesh, the Second Person of the Trinity. These latter affirmations reflect the hard-won development of the doctrine of the church over many centuries. But this development rests on the firm foundation of the life of Jesus of Nazareth, this marginal Jew who lived and died in Palestine in the first century of our era, an era named after him. We have seen that he was a mystery even in his own time, a man with a mysterious and awesome relationship with God, a man who inspired awe in those who met him and who saw him in action. But it was only in his crucifixion, death, and resurrection that he was truly seen by the eyes of faith as who he really was and is, the only begotten Son of God, the Word made flesh, the Holy One of God, our Savior and Redeemer.

In this book we have asked to know Jesus better in order to love him more and to follow him more closely. In the last chapter we also asked to have compassion for him in his sufferings, to experience with him what he underwent during his last week of ordinary life. I hope that this book has been a help to attain that desire. Perhaps now we might want to ask Jesus to share with us the joy of his resurrection as he shared it with his disciples. We can give him a chance to share with us his joy by using the stories of his resurrection appearances in the same contemplative way we used the stories of his life in Palestine.

Let me end with some reflections that might help us in developing our relationship with Jesus. Jesus died in the prime of his life. Just as he never experienced the joys and sorrows of married and family life, he never got to experience the joys and pains of middle age and of growing old. In addition, his experience was limited to his own time and place. In other words, many experiences that we have are foreign to him. Just as he needed disciples during his lifetime to share his ministry, so too, I believe, he needs followers now who will carry on his work.

Might it not also be true that he relies on our willingness to reveal ourselves to him to experience those aspects of life that could not be packed into his own earthly life? This might be another reason for engaging in a mutual relationship of friendship with Jesus. Not only does it help us to be able to tell Jesus the intimate details of our lives, but it may also be enlightening to him, as a (risen) human being, to hear what it is like for us to live our lives in wholly different circumstances. At the least, by letting him know what we are experiencing we are showing a trust in him, a trust not only that he will listen with sympathy and empathy but also that he wants to be our friend. The gospel of John puts these words into the mouth of Jesus at the Last Supper. It may be a fitting ending to this book to hear them as addressed to us:

> I do not call you servants any longer, because the servant does not know what the master is doing; but I have called you friends, because I have made known to you everything that I have heard from my Father. You did not choose me but I chose you. And I appointed you to go and bear fruit, fruit that will last, so that the Father will give you whatever you ask him in my name. I am giving you these commands so that you may love one another (John 15:15-17).

Bibliography

Barclay, William, *The Gospel of Mark: Revised Edition*. Philadelphia: Westminster, 1975.

Barry, William A., *Spiritual Direction and the Encounter with God*. New York/Mahwah: Paulist, 1992.

Barry, William A., *What Do I Want in Prayer?* New York/Mahwah: Paulist, 1994.

Bernanos, Georges, *The Diary of a Country Priest*. Trans. Pamela Morris. New York: Carroll & Graf, 1983.

Brown, Raymond E., *The Death of the Messiah: From Gethsemane to the Grave: A Commentary on the Passion Narratives in the Four Gospels*. Two volumes. New York: Doubleday, 1994.

Brown, Raymond E., *An Introduction to New Testament Christology*. New York/Mahwah: Paulist, 1994.

Brown, Raymond E., "The Twelve and the Apostolate," *NJBC*, 1377-81.

Brown, Raymond E., Joseph A. Fitzmyer, and Roland E. Murphy, eds., *The New Jerome Biblical Commentary*. Englewood Cliffs, NJ: Prentice Hall, 1990. (In the text and in the bibliography listed as *NJBC*.)

Buechner, Frederick, *Love Feast, Part III of the Book of Bebb*. San Francisco: Harper & Row, 1984.

DiGiacomo, Susan M., "The Case: A Narrative Deconstruction of 'Diagnostic Delay,'" *Second Opinion*, 20, no. 4 (April 1995), 21-35.

Eadie, Betty J. (with Curtis Taylor), *Embraced by the Light*. Placerville, CA: Gold Leaf Press, 1992.

Endo, Shusaku, *A Life of Jesus*. Trans. Richard A. Schuchert. New York/Mahwah: Paulist, 1978.

Fitzmyer, Joseph A., "A History of Israel: From Pompey to Bar Cochba," *NJBC*, 1243-52.

Furlong, Monica, "Busy as a Bluebottle," *The Tablet*, March 4, 1995.

Gies, Martha, "A Heart of Wisdom," *Second Opinion* 20, no. 4 (April 1995), 11-19.

Gill, David, "Making Sense of Martyrdom, *Human Development* 12, no. 3 (Fall 1991), 44-47.

147

Goggins, Gerard E., *Anonymous Disciple*. Worcester, MA: Assumption Communications, 1995.

Haight, Roger, "Jesus and Mission: An Overview of the Problem," *Discovery: Jesuit International Missions* 5 (December 1994.)

Harrington, Daniel J., *The Gospel of Matthew*. Collegeville, MN: Liturgical Press, 1991.

Hengel, Martin, *The Charismatic Leader and His Followers*. New York: Crossroad, 1981.

Hillesum, Etty, *An Interrupted Life: The Diaries of Etty Hillesum*, 1941-43. New York: Washington Square Press, 1985.

Hollings, Michael, "The Lourdes Effect," *The Tablet* (June 17, 1995) 771-72.

Julian of Norwich, *Revelations of Divine Love*. Rev. ed. Ed. Marion Glasscoe. Exeter: University of Exeter Press, 1993.

Kelly, Kevin, "Living with HIV/AIDS," *The Tablet* (May 13, 1995) 597-99.

Macmurray, John, *The Form of the Personal*. Volume I: *The Self as Agent*; Volume II: *Persons in Relation*. Atlantic Highlands, NJ: Humanities Press, 1969.

Meier, John P., "Jesus," *NJBC*, 1316-28.

Meier, John P., *A Marginal Jew: Rethinking the Historical Jesus*. Volume One: *The Roots of the Problem and the Person*; Volume Two: *Mentor, Message, and Miracles*. New York: Doubleday, 1991, 1994.

Murphy-O'Connor, Jerome, "The First Letter to the Corinthians," *NJBC*, 798-815.

Price, Reynolds, *A Whole New Life*. New York: Atheneum, 1994.

Rosengarten, Theodore, *All God's Dangers: The Life of Nate Shaw*. New York: Knopf, 1974.

E. P. Sanders, *The Historical Figure of Jesus*. London: Penguin, 1993.

Schüssler-Fiorenza, Elizabeth, *In Memory of Her: A Feminist Theological Reconstruction of Christian Origins*. New York: Crossroads, 1983.

Whitfield, Teresa, *Paying the Price: Ignacio Ellacuría and the Murdered Jesuits of El Salvador*. Philadelphia: Temple University Press, 1995.